AD Biography
Labro Phi 1997

Labro, Philippe, 1936 – Dark tunnel, white light
: my journey to death and beyond   9000809487

ourne

12/
97

9000809487

DISCARDED BY
MEAD PUBLIC LIBRARY

Dark Tunnel, White Light

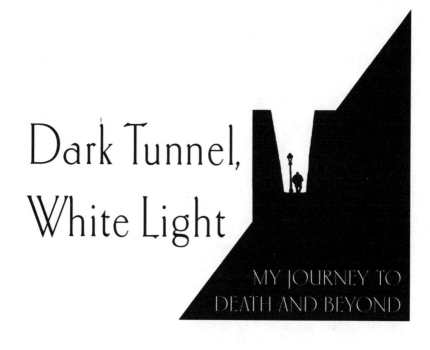

Dark Tunnel,
White Light

MY JOURNEY TO
DEATH AND BEYOND

PHILIPPE LABRO
Translated by Linda Coverdale

KODANSHA INTERNATIONAL
New York • Tokyo • London

Kodansha America, Inc.
114 Fifth Avenue, New York, New York 10011, U.S.A.

Kodansha International Ltd.
17-14 Otowa 1-chome, Bunkyo-ku, Tokyo 112, Japan

Published in 1997 by Kodansha America, Inc.

Copyright © 1997 by Philippe Labro
English translation © 1997 by Linda Coverdale
All rights reserved.

Library of Congress Cataloging-in-Publication Data

Labro, Philippe.
    [Traversée. English]
    Dark tunnel, white light : my journey to death and beyond /
  Philippe Labro ; translated by Linda Coverdale.
       p.   cm.
     1. Labro, Philippe—Health.   2. Authors, French—20th century—
  Health and hygiene.   3. Near-death experiences.   I. Title.
PQ2672.A22Z4713   1997
843'.914—dc21
[B]
ISBN 1-56836-200-5   97-25405
                                             CIP

Book design by Helene Berinsky

Manufactured in the United States of America

97 98 99 00   10 9 8 7 6 5 4 3 2 1

KO9482

809487

To my mother

*In the early morning on the lake
sitting in the stern of the boat with
his father rowing, he felt quite sure
that he would never die.*

—ERNEST HEMINGWAY

Dark Tunnel, White Light

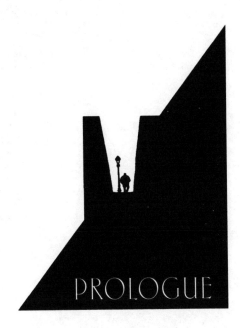

PROLOGUE

The Visitors

THEY ARE STANDING close together, in a single straight line along the white wall (or is it light yellow?), and they are all smiling. Their eyes, their gestures, their faces express a strange eagerness, almost an invitation. Everything about their friendly attitude seems intended to tell me, "Come on!"

One of them, the oldest man, finally speaks and says precisely what I'd seemed to hear: "Come on!" Then he adds, "Come and join us. We're expecting you."

As though the matter were settled, a foregone conclusion. I look at the little group lined up in front of the wall. Some are old, some are young. I see a fat man, a thin one, a woman with red hair, a black woman, a blonde, two rather slender young men, some elderly people. A few are wearing glasses; one has on a big white hat. I know them so well!

The women are smiling, like the men. I love them all, these men and women. There are no more than a dozen of them. I have loved

3

them all, but they are dead, and I still love them, since they live on in my memory. They are the dead of my life. I wonder why I should join them. I hadn't planned on it. Nevertheless, they insist. They all seem to have adopted the same frank countenance and open smile, the same slightly oppressive, slightly wearing pleasantness. Their gentleness is persistent, insidious, cloying.

"Well, come on! What are you waiting for?"

A gentleness in slow motion, like their gestures, which are few and deliberate. They know what they're doing and what they want, and I find that a bit annoying. Because even though I love them, I don't like their insistence, their smugness, that sort of affected solemnity they have, their certainty that it's going to work and I'm going to obey them and cross the line! No: they are dead. I don't want to go there.

I just said that they are dead, but they aren't dead since I am alive and they are right there, as large as life in front of the white-yellow wall, and talking to me. Or could it be that I'm the one who isn't alive anymore?

They remain almost motionless, facing me, on the other side, not far, barely a yard away, but I'm not going to join them. I don't want to. Do I have a choice? Is it a duty, a command? What do they want of me and what is that god-awful noise shuddering through me? I look away from those people standing there, I shift my gaze a few degrees, and now I can't see the people by the wall at all. Suddenly, the room is flooded with blue. Because I'm in a room, I'm on a bed, and I am shocked by the profusion of tubes sticking out of my face.

And all of a sudden, waves of blue forests appear.

Why?

Reason Is Not Always Right

AT THE FOOT OF DOLORES PEAK, in the thick of the Uncompahgre forest, there is a geological fault, a long, flat, rugged promontory of naked rock cleft in the center as though by a giant ax. The Ute Indians, who inhabited the area well before the arrival of the white man, named this spot "the Eagle's Notch." It isn't easy to get to the Notch, but all who have managed to reach it come back changed. They have seen. They have seen a sea of unparalleled depth and beauty.

It is a sea of fir trees, blue-green, green-blue. It ripples before your eyes like a vast, endless carpet of blue velvet shot through with every other color—lavender, lemon, ocher, jet black, purple, and carmine—but dominated by the blue that absorbs them all into its immobile yet shimmering undulation. The sky above this sea, unlike all others, is often of a lighter blue, faded and pure, unmixed with further tints. The combination of these two blues—the dark and iridescent carpet, and the limpid, transparent backdrop of the sky—imbues this vision with a seductive power that is almost magical, and possibly fatal.

A local legend says, in fact, that if you gaze down too intently at this sea, you may succumb to the temptation to plunge into it, to lose yourself there. People also say that certain animals have given in to this temptation, as have certain men, perhaps, and that no one has ever found a trace of their bodies, even after searching for several days through the undergrowth beneath the towering trees of the Uncompahgre.

I WOULD LIKE to tell you about something that happened to me not too long ago, something that occurred not in those Colorado mountains I've just described, but in the more everyday context of the city where I live, in Paris, and more precisely in a tiny space within the four walls of various rooms in a big hospital in that same city. What happened changed my life . . . since I almost lost it! For a reason that might at first seem obscure and complicated, but that will turn out to be quite simple, and that I only discovered on the day when I decided to tell my story, I cannot begin to do so without speaking of the Eagle's Notch and the thousands of blue-crested waves, the thousands of firs resembling that ocean in which, with my friends, when I was eighteen years old, I once wanted to melt away.

As a matter of fact, this image appeared to me—after one of the visitors lined up close together in my room—when I awakened from the first anesthesia in the hospital, and it's the image that came perhaps most often to my mind, into my thoughts, throughout the long stationary voyage I made on that hospital bed, a voyage that carried me to death's door.

Everything is connected, everything fits together. If this unforgettable image is at the very heart of a story that unfolds years and miles away from that hospital room, it's because there exists a reason that has nothing to do with Reason.

Grown-ups believe one can explain everything by calling on Reason. I've learned not to pass judgment in that way. Actually, I've learned not to pass judgment too much at all. I try only to understand. Life is a mystery, time is a mystery, each of us obeys different laws, and Reason does not constitute the Law. I often find it hard to say these things before those who cling excessively to Reason, because they then look at me with that vacant stare that signals the incomprehension, indeed even the condescension, of those who rely exclusively on their intelligence to understand life and the world. I no longer have any trouble these days in establishing the difference between Reason and everything else. It wasn't only Reason or intelligence that played a role in what happened to me, but other, much stronger elements as well: willpower, love, heart, the unexpected.

My story is not a tale of make-believe, a work of fiction, so to tell it I'd like to use words that are simple, authentic, and sincere— but I must first return to the Eagle's Notch.

A Sea of Blue Firs

THE EAGLE'S NOTCH! The image recurs constantly, now that I am gradually emerging from my anesthetized limbo. I'm still completely unaware of my body and of all the trammels and restraints that have been placed upon it. I'm haunted by this one particular image. Why?

THERE WERE a few of us, in the camp at the foot of the mountain, who were intrigued by this notch. If you reached it, we were told, you felt something strange, unique, something you couldn't ever experience through alcohol, love, violence, or dreams. A man had told us so, and we believed it. There were three or four of us who wanted to believe it and to find out about this unknown sensation. The man who had first mentioned it to us had said, "You must be worthy of the Eagle's Notch."

He was an old man of mixed white and Indian blood, and he was called Red Cloud, a name passed down from glorious ancestors. He didn't work in the camp, but brought us our mail and a few provisions once a week in his ancient, battered Ford pickup. He was so old that his wrinkles had tributaries of other wrinkles, just as rivers gather in streams. He'd noticed the group of youths, myself among them, who in the evening twilight, during the last leisurely half hour after our six o'clock supper (we ate early so as to go to bed early and get up early), used to sit on the grassy butte where the tents were pitched above the river, gazing up at Dolores Peak, toward the Notch. Red Cloud had come over to join us.

"You want to go up there?"

"How did you know?" one of my friends had replied.

Red Cloud had smiled—or at least I'd thought I'd seen a smile on that tanned and weathered face, as seamed as parched clay—but he hadn't answered the question, since it was a foolish one. How do you know what goes on in the heads of young people? You know because you're older than they are.

"You'll have to leave early," he'd said, "because it takes longer than you think. Pack along food and plenty to drink. Follow the Beaver Trail, right to the foot of the peak. Then all you have to do is climb, but try not to get too cut up. That rock is hard on skin."

"How about if we use gloves?" one of us had asked.

Red Cloud had burst out laughing.

"No, don't bother wearing gloves."

We'd followed his advice and set out in the predawn chill, walking in icy darkness while the wind off the mountain shook the ponderosa pines all around us, enveloping us in their heady, resinous scent. It felt good to climb at that easy pace toward the borderline where the trees would soon disappear, leaving us on arid, scree-covered slopes. Twigs and pine needles crunched underfoot, and we could sense the unseen presence of rodents and insects allowing man to pass by their mossy refuges, their dens beneath the ferns, the stumps and trunks of felled trees, the corpses of firs uprooted by ancient deluges, lightning bolts, and gales that had tried to destroy the forest only to whirl on their way, dispersed into the empty air. The forest, gashed and wounded, had endured. No storm was strong enough to beat that forest down.

WHY DO THESE DETAILS come back to me with such precision? These colors, these sounds, in the yellow room where I saw the visitors lined up in a row, beckoning me to join them . . . Why am I so determined to reconstruct our hike to the Eagle's Notch?

WE FINALLY CAME to the bare rock itself. The sun was just peeking over the horizon, throwing a rosy, silken veil over the black night sky. We quickly found ourselves stooped over, moving along on all fours, like the lynx and mountain lion prowling not far away. The slope was too steep for us to proceed any farther walking upright. The air was dry and powdery, and we had to take deep, even breaths. We climbed for two hours. The sun was beating down on us now, and it was strange to feel both the chill of the everlasting snows and the warmth—not really the heat—of the sun. We stopped frequently, drinking from our canteens and moistening the cloth bands inside our hats to keep the backs of our necks cool and avoid sunstroke. We knew sunstroke was unlikely, because of the cold, but we were still afraid of it. Red Cloud had been right: our hands were bloody.

When we reached the top, I felt as though I'd crossed an invisible barrier, passing from a world of warmth and reality into one completely outside the realm of ordinary existence. Before us lay the massive, broken slab: smooth, naked, tipped slightly up into the sky, so that you had to lie down flat on it. The wind was fierce. A feeling of vertigo—or at least of constant disequilibrium—naturally led you to stretch out on the rock. Then you crawled on your stomach toward the cleft and the void, anxious to find out about that sea, eager to contemplate that carpet at last.

So there was the void. The winds that went right to your head and all that blue rippling below us, that beauty, that purity of things and time, and that disturbing longing we might begin to feel—the longing to plunge into the sea and become part of it. To roll around on that carpet, if it was one, as a child rolls on a bed or a baby on its mother's lap. That longing to become one forever with the beauty and the color of that great beyond, that different world you seemed to hear calling to you, "Come on!"

I'M NOT STRETCHED OUT on that rocky slab in the Uncompah-gre at all, however, and I'm not eighteen anymore, and many, many years have passed, but the blue is there, rippling, before my eyes. And yet I'm lying in a room with white—or yellow—walls and I can see once again a group of men, of women. . . . They are the dead of my life and they have said to me, "Come on!"

What is this noise rushing through me?

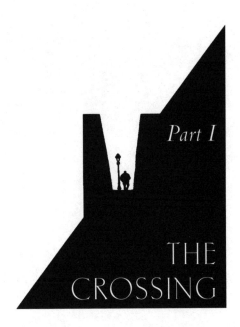

Part I

THE
CROSSING

The ICU

THE NOISE WAS COMING from a machine called a mechanical respirator. This device pumps air through a silicone tube inserted into the trachea so that the patient can breathe.

The patient knew nothing of all this. He heard only the sound of the machine and the sound of his own breathing—irregular, gasping, hacking—while in his mouth, a tube as slender as an insignificant little wire felt even bigger than a bear's paw. He was lying on a bed, his arms fastened to the side rails with Velcro strips.

He could feel that his lips, his nose, his cheeks had been fitted out with all sorts of ties, pieces of adhesive tape, and gauze pads—a rig that immobilized him as securely as the intravenous drip attached to his left forearm, or the electrodes taped on his chest and linked to a cardiac monitor on which, had he been able to see it, he would have noticed a green line: his heartline.

He hadn't seen anything when he had awakened, actually. He emerged from a dark and chaotic reverie believing that he had been brought to this room at the end of the hall—the last room in the building, as they'd explained to him—accompanied by his wife, the doctors, and the interns, and he was convinced that they'd sung hymns when they moved him there and that those in the procession had carried candles, as though for a funeral cortège. He was coming to, still groggy from the anesthetic. And he wasn't in pain. But if he had been able to reconstruct clearly the events preceding his arrival in the room, he would have summed them up this way:

"You hadn't been able to breathe normally for a long while. That cough of yours was now a habit. Soon your larynx became obstructed. It affected your daily life. You lost weight, and sleep, and your health suffered. You tried too many doctors, too many medications, and the specialist you consulted now and then finally said, 'I cannot continue treating you like this, you'll have to go into the hospital.' You refused for a long time—a long time, two days!—and in the end you called the specialist to say, 'I'm ready.' These were the only words you could still say, since the edema blocking the opening of your larynx was on the verge of choking you. You went into the hospital. They put you to sleep to perform a bronchoscopy on you, and now you find yourself here, but what condition are you in? And what is this *here*?"

Here is the Intensive Care Unit. The ICU, as it's called in the hospital. The ICU: a universe, a world with its own rules, codes, atmosphere, colors, sounds—all related to illness and to the treatment given those who are ill.

Everyone who has been in intensive care knows what those three little letters mean, and surely countless sufferers have endured longer and more agonizing trials there than I did. And surely the experience of still others was less cruel than mine. It's different for each of us, this ICU "crossing." Nevertheless, this crossing, provided you survive it, gives you a little extra dose of experience, a little additional knowledge. Oh, it's nothing much, almost as insubstantial as the sigh of a dragonfly among rustling reeds, but all the same, you're no longer the person you were before the ICU. You've crossed to the other side, you've rounded Cape Horn.

These expressions may seem banal. "Crossing to the other side," what a cliché! "Rounding Cape Horn," what a trite image! Such criticism should be brushed off. If the image seems facile, it's because it's the right image. The problem isn't writing "the other side," but trying to describe what it's like, and affirming this first of all: there is another side.

This Is Not a Novel

THE ILLNESS THAT LED ME to the ICU took me past it, well beyond Cape Horn, beyond the Roaring Forties and the Screaming Fifties, into what is called a near-death experience: NDE.

During this crossing, I saw and heard all sorts of things. Monsters, angels, faces and landscapes, emptiness and excess, compassion, horror, and love. While I was struggling with a constant disruption of time and duration, when days and nights no longer had any meaning, any structure, when I had lost all frame of reference and was summoning up moments from both my past and my life to come. While two of me carried on a constant argument in which one self would say, "You're going to die, let go, you're finished," and the other self would insist, "No, keep fighting, you've got to live."

The texture and weave of this confrontation and this dialogue (unheard by anyone, but that I can transcribe line for line), these moments of an unreal present and a past recalled to life, my two

NDEs—one bathed in light, the other teetering on the edge of a dark precipice—and all that followed, which is to say a kind of rebirth, and all that still remains today of these discoveries and convictions, are what I hope to recapture, and set before you.

WHEN I LEFT the hospital after six weeks—ten days in the ICU, the rest in a room—I was torn between the desire to talk about my crossing and the equally strong wish to keep silent. It was summertime. I was coasting along, occasionally leaving the forest where I was recuperating for a little foray into Paris. I was talkative or silent, depending on my company and the time of day. I'd feel like hugging complete strangers, chatting their ears off, and then I'd want to go off on my own and not say another word. This ambivalence didn't last long. One day B., the radiologist who was giving me a routine examination, asked me some questions, and we got to talking. In a warm, encouraging voice, he said, "You ought to write about all that."

B. is a big, solid guy, with black hair and a clear gaze. He wears glasses with light, almost transparent frames. I quite like him, but he probably doesn't know this. In the first place, I've never told him so. And then I've only met him about a dozen times, whenever I've gone to his office to have X-rays taken. He's young, alert, direct and concise in his evaluation of the X-rays, and he exudes that ease, that sincerity so characteristic of certain Algerian-born French with whom I've always felt a rapport and whose friendship has accompanied me through my journeys, my various careers, and a war. When I talk to him, I feel as though I were speaking with the brother of all those men with whom I've witnessed explosions, riots, or floods; with whom I've covered trials or royal weddings; with whom I've written scenarios and shot films; with whom, at night, when I was young, in Paris, New York, or Los Angeles, I fooled around, cut up, ran wild. He's the brother of the other men I talk to every day—or almost every day, no matter what else is going on—about what we've read, done, seen, or how those close to us are doing. B. belongs to a vast anonymous family. It seems we all know what it's like to cherish kindred spirits outside our private world, men and women who don't move in the same circles. Since my stay in the ICU, I've felt more open to this feeling of fraternity.

After going over the X-ray and recording his analysis on a dictaphone the size and shape of a cigarette pack, after telling me that everything looks fine, B. questions me, and since our relationship is a friendly one, I describe what I discovered about myself and about "the other side."

"You ought to write about it," he says again.

"Everybody tells me the same thing. I want to, and then I don't want to. Almost a year has gone by. I don't know. I'm neither the first nor the last to have suffered, to have crossed over to the other side and come back. It's not as exceptional as all that."

"But that's not true. It isn't your suffering that interests us, it's the rest of it, that great unknown you came so close to and that most people haven't ever experienced. Tell about it in your own words, plain and simple."

I hadn't needed B., with his warm voice and candid eyes, to tell me it was time to tackle this narrative. I'd made some notes, and I didn't think I should keep that recurrent image of the Colorado firs—or its attendant images, those visions, sensations, transformations—to myself. I was beating around the bush, somewhat the way I'm doing now on this page, warily circling my recent experience, still keeping a few sentences between myself and the story. Because I'd gone back to my usual surroundings, my job, my routines. Nothing erases the ordeal, however. Not once you've rounded Cape Horn. Really, can you and should you just forget about something like that? Of course not.

Even if mind and body allow themselves to become caught up in everyday life again, and even if you find your demons waiting for you, along with your faults—your pettiness and selfishness—as well as your former interests, impulses, passions, and plans, you still aren't exactly the same person anymore. This great upheaval deserves to be described without fiction, without fantasy, without distortions, without lies.

The writer I tried to be in my previous novels must bow out this time, and stay out. I've always shuffled things around in my writing, and that was normal, the usual work of a novelist. I used my life as material for my books and I invented things that were based on my life. Some people thought I was telling the story of my life just as it had happened, with scrupulous fidelity. Which wasn't the case. This time, I am not writing a novel.

What you will say is true. It all happened. And even if you have to speak of something that did not happen—you lived it as if it had. So, it did happen.

The Most Important Women in My Life

FIRST OF ALL, there are the women. I live in a world run by women, rather young ones. Most of the time, when I discover them, there are two of them. Later, they will separate, then get back together, and I'll be entitled to only one of them, but when I first see them, there are two.

They wear outfits of a lightweight, green material. They have masks over their mouths, they talk to each other, and they talk about "him"—that is, me—as if I weren't in the room. Perhaps they think I can't hear them. It's true that I don't always hear them and that what I think I hear them saying isn't necessarily what they've said.

They are quick, but not rushed; they are meticulous. They have work to do, tasks to perform. These are women who will never, even for a single instant, appear before my eyes—half-closed, semi-comatose, but my eyes all the same—in a moment of idleness or relaxation. When I see them, they will always be busy: tending, safeguarding, saving, and guarding. They are always, always doing something. They divide up the duties after studying sheets of instructions and establishing the plan of care for each patient. They decide which of them will look after which patient, since they are clearly responsible for more than one bed. And so, although I am completely obsessed with my fate alone, shaken by surging fears of my danger alone, I will, thanks to these young women's words, realize that I am not the only inhabitant of the ICU. There are other cubicles, the sounds that I hear are not always those of "my machine," and the bells that alert the young women aren't all connected to the call button within reach of my hand. I will eventually sense that there is someone in the room right next door. I will gather that his name is Mr. Picolino or Picolini, and judging from the time the young women devote to him, I will realize that Mr. Picolino or Picolini is doing very poorly and causing great concern.

For brief moments, by opening my eyes wide, by straining to peer through a film of tears, I can manage to see the chart the young woman still in the room has hung up on the wall over her work counter. There are spaces marked with a black, green, or red triangle. Each square corresponds to a task: giving medication, checking blood pressure, checking temperature, taking a blood sample, cleaning the tube that ties you to the respirator, and checking the machine, the IV drip, the saline, the dosage, and the rate.

The women will change with each shift—three sets of two, who work in three eight-hour stretches—and these abrupt appearances of new couples and names, fresh faces and voices, will provide the only reference points to gauge the passage of time. Time is a thread that breaks frequently, tangles and snarls, becomes lost, and cannot be found again. Only the nurses allow you to go on understanding that there are hours, days, nights. Of course, the light that bathes the room—to the right, up there on the wall, there's something like a skylight or those little barred windows in prisons—gives you the idea that it's daytime, and when the fluorescent fixtures on the ceiling come on, you will dimly understand that this day has just ended. But if the nurses did not change, with new names, new accents, new faces, you would have no idea of the passage of a time anything like the one you had known until then, in a normal existence. So the nurses are, among other things, your clock, your only explanation of time. But they are more than that. The ICU nurses have become the most important women in your life.

I NEED THESE WOMEN the way I've never needed anyone before. I depend on them completely. I feel that my life lies in their hands, that my life depends on theirs. Only they know how to comfort me.

When the strongest effects of the anesthetic had begun to wear off after the bronchoscopy, after my awakening, after the visit from my dead loved ones and the visions of the sky and forests of Colorado, after I had realized that the infernal noise was coming from that machine to which I was tethered by the tube that had taken over my mouth and windpipe, and after I had vaguely—but only vaguely!—absorbed the small amount of information a man in white (Well! A man!) had come to give me, bending over me and insisting that I respond by nodding my head, since I couldn't speak anymore because of the intubation, I grasped this one reality: these nurses who come, go, work, talk, and fall silent are your sole resource. Your only hope. You constantly feel as though you were drowning. They alone can hold your head above water. You feel as though you were perpetually burning in a fire that they alone can extinguish. But only for the time being. Because the fire flares up again, regularly, and the drowning begins again, just as regularly. So you will call them continually, endlessly pressing with your left hand on that little button—your link with the world—that will once more turn on a blinking light over the door to the room and set off a short, repetitive beeping, an unpleasant and intolerable *dit-dit-dit-dit* that will, once again, bring one of the young women back into the room to turn off the light and the bell, come over to you, where you lie imprisoned by your bonds and your silence and ask, yet another time, "What's wrong? What do you want? What can I do for you?"

Then you will—by wiggling your wrist (feebly, given the tiny amount of space available for wiggling, since your wrist is tied to the side rail), by wagging your head, by trying to talk with your eyes—attempt to make her understand that the tube is clogged, that it's harder for you to breathe, that you think you're going to choke on what is coming up from your bronchi, and that you can't manage to breathe with the machine anymore. You're not in sync with the machine, which now sets off its own alarm. Another bell rings—more frenetically, more unbearably, a true siren of catastrophe—and the young nurse will understand and speak the words you've been waiting for.

"Okay, I'm going to suction you, don't worry."

She will "suction" you. That's the term they all use. It's not very pretty, not very elegant, but in the world of the ICU, there is no room for elegant language. Here, words are clear, concrete, precise. They call a spade a spade, and a tube a tube. And *suctioning* means just what it says: after quickly and temporarily disconnecting the ventilator tube, the nurse, using a kind of catheter, vacuums your whole throat, your palate, your trachea, sucking up that thick, fluid material responsible for the horrible, suffocating feeling. The young woman suctions you. It's noisy, it's painful, but it's a pain that releases you from a different pain and thus does you some good. She replaces the ties that hold the tube in place, and once more you feel, briefly, relieved. She settles your head back on the pillow and takes a moment to adjust your position in the bed as well. You look at her and hope she can tell from your eyes how much you want her to stay with you and not go off again to take care of Mr. Picolino or Picolini, and how much you admire the speed with which she helped you, allowing you to keep going.

Then, since you cannot express a single one of these feelings, you signal with two fingers of your right hand to indicate that you want to write something. The nurse catches on quickly. They understand these gestures, they know how to read signs. They've been through this scene so many times. They are not assigned to the ICU by accident. In general, they last no more than two or three years there. It's tough work. Emotionally draining. Some of the patients die. There is constant stress. Some girls, they say, manage to carry on only because they know that they are helping, that the work they do makes a real difference. They are volunteers. They are not assigned to the ICU unless they have chosen to go there and been picked for the job. So they know what you want. They hand you a tiny plastic tablet and a felt-tip pen with which you slowly write (it's funny how you have such trouble writing—won't your fingers ever get their strength back?) two words: thank you.

The young woman reads your message. "You're welcome," she murmurs. "I hope you'll feel better now."

She turns to leave the room. When she darts a look at you, after erasing the message, putting back the pen and tablet, and writing a remark in the nurse's notes, you think you can read a question in her eyes. As if she were wondering, "Why would he be thanking me?"

In Which We Are Introduced
to Karen the Korean

HE WAS UNABLE to figure out how long it had taken him to identify each nurse by her first name. He thought he knew almost all of
them: Patricia, Elizabeth, Chantal, Catherine, Fabienne, Bénédicte,
Nathalie. And on the night shifts, there was a Korean named Karen.

She was prettier than the others. She had brown hair (rather in-
expertly cut), a fine complexion, full lips, long eyelashes, and high
cheekbones. She seemed coquettish, self-involved, susceptible to the
flattery lavished on her by her coworker on the night shift, a small,
chubby young woman with short hair and an accent from the south-
east of France, perhaps from around Béziers. The two nurses were
an odd couple: they did their work, of course, but unlike the other
nurses, they gave him the impression that this work wasn't their pri-
mary concern. They chattered quite a bit, telling each other about
their private lives; one of them, the less attractive and outgoing of
the two, listened to the romantic troubles of the other—Karen the

Korean—and gave her to understand that she'd made a mistake in choosing men. Women were better.

It seemed to him that Karen was neither very skillful nor particularly professional. The first time he'd seen her come into the room at night to begin her shift and consult the doctor's orders, he'd heard her commenting out loud about all the things she'd have to do during the next eight hours.

"Oh, no! There's so much to do! I'll never be able to finish all that, never."

Her voice sounded common to him, and didn't seem to go with her Asian starlet appearance.

"Don't worry about it, Karen," said the other nurse. "I'm here—I'll explain things to you, and I can help you out and do the hardest parts. I'll take care of this, this, and this. Then we can both take a break and you can tell me all about your boyfriends and it'll be fine, you'll see. We've got the whole night ahead of us. We'll get everything organized. We're not going to let *him* bother us!"

He listened uneasily, dumbfounded, struggling with his pain, his tube, his coughing, his machine, its sounds and cadences, and he thought he detected in the nurses' dialogue the beginning or the prolongation of some intrigue or other on the ICU night shift. They were blithely living a life that didn't revolve around him!

But Karen suddenly rebelled.

"I'll figure it out by myself. You know, I do what I want with my life. I make my own choices."

The other nurse seemed let down, and replied with the dry tone of a disappointed suitor.

"Whatever you like, Karen, suit yourself."

Karen turned her back on the other woman. She seemed intent on paying more attention to her instructions, the medications to be administered, the plans of care to be set up, the IVs to be hung. But he could hear her talking to herself.

"That little bitch, that little bitch, she won't get me like that, I've got better things to do!"

The sick man felt a mounting anxiety stronger than any he'd already experienced since awakening in the ICU. Was he going to end up victimized by the mood swings of two nurses? How could they take care of him if the place turned into a circus? He was restless, even more sensitive to the painful thudding in his chest and throughout his body. He thought he should fight against drowsiness, against that sort of sporadic, disjointed sleep that racked his nights. What passed for sleep in his present state. He told himself that this would be one of the most agonizing and exhausting nights he'd had since his arrival.

But the private life of Karen the Korean was not the only reason for this growing anguish. The truth is, at about the same time, he had finally realized that he had a very good chance of dying.

The First Principle of the Crossing

YOU REALIZE THAT you may die when you learn that no one has yet discovered precisely what is wrong with you. So no one has found a remedy to get you out of the hole you're in. You become aware of the hole.

And it's endless. Disorienting. Like nothing else. Indescribable. Interminable. No pain you've ever felt before in your life even comes close to that one. The hole is noisy, because of the respirator, the rhythm of which speeds up crazily whenever your breathing becomes panicky and a coughing fit disturbs the mechanical cycle. Alarms go off. Doors open, nurses arrive, sometimes even the intern on duty shows up.

"Just learn to work with the machine, *monsieur*. It's an excellent machine. Adjust yourself to it. Work with it."

"Work with the machine!" You hate that machine. You don't understand that without it, you would already have suffocated and been subjected to a tracheotomy. This machine, this hole, these intimations of the abyss, everything suggests that things aren't going well, not one bit, and above all, there are those other faces. They explain things to you, talk to you, tell you that they're trying to identify what they think is a rare, abnormal bacterium that has severely compromised your respiratory system, and that this is why they keep drawing so much blood from you. At least six times a day, to obtain microbes and do hemocultures. They tell you six, but it seems to you that it never stops. That the passing hours are punctuated by needles in your veins. That all they do is take your blood, that your time is devoted entirely to that: needles going in, blood going out. The worst is when they say, "We're going to check your blood gases," and they say that often.

You don't understand. They can tell from your eyes that you'd like to know what's going on.

"It's to check the balance of oxygen and carbon dioxide, evaluate the severity of the pulmonary dysfunction, and make sure the ventilation is adequate."

For the "blood gases," they don't use a vein in the forearm, where they usually draw blood, but a smaller, more specific spot in an artery within the wrist. It's much more painful, sharp, and deep. Since they don't want to cause a hematoma, the nurse presses her thumb down quite hard on the artery after drawing the blood. It hurts a lot, this blood gases business, it really hurts a lot. And you wonder, will there ever be an end to all this?

AN END, but what end? Another face, a woman's face, helps me understand that perhaps it will come to an end. Until that moment, befuddled by the lingering effects of the anesthetic, by the bombardment of images assailing me, by the discovery of everything imprisoning me (tubes, IV drip, the respirator with its mechanical rhythms), I had seen mostly women's faces, true, but they were the faces of strangers. They were comforting women, since they demonstrated their ability to help me, watch over me, and relieve my pain. And they reassured me, of course, with a few, simple words repeated over and over again: "Don't worry, we'll take care of you."

In the eyes, the smiles, the gestures of these women, I saw only messages of encouragement. It was in the face of the woman dearest to me that I read a different message.

Because the face I had so longed to see appears at last. For the first time. My wife has come to speak to me in our private language, in her own words. Words filled with love. She talks, and talks, and talks to me. I'm unable to reply. Since I know this face better than all those others that have leaned over mine, I think I can read more deeply into it. First I see gentleness, affection, solicitude, and love. I see it all: our whole past, the children, the years of complicity and understanding, sharing all things at all times. I am able, thanks to her, to feel a warm emotion that isn't the harsh heat of the fire that courses regularly through my body, but a soothing warmth that has restored to me, for a brief moment, what I have missed most of all since I came to the ICU: a sense of well-being.

"You can speak to him," the doctors had told her, "but he won't hear you. He doesn't hear much."

But she didn't listen to the doctors. Like all those who love and who find themselves in a hospital at the bedside of the one they love, she spoke from her heart. She thought, "He'll hear me. Something will surely get through to him out of everything I'm going to say, even if it makes only the slightest impression, and he'll know that I'm here."

I do hear her. Like many women, she knows that kindness and love can pierce the chemical cloud, cross the technological barrier. And even if she doesn't really know this, she means to try.

Her love does reach me. A small dose of well-being, but small as it is, its effect is almost too powerful. I quickly feel breathless, overcome. I gesture weakly, trying to signal that it's too much for me to take in, that this excess of emotion is overwhelming me. I'm not strong enough to savor a moment of happiness. What amazes me is that she understands what is happening.

"You want me to go, right?" she asks immediately. "You want me to leave you alone?"

I nod. I would like to cry out, "It's not because I don't want to see you, it's because I simply can't bear to. It's not because I don't love you, it's because I love you too much. And right at this moment, loving too much takes my breath away. It's because I love you that you must take away your hand, your eyes, your face, your gaze—all these images before me must go away, because I just can't bear it. I don't want you to go, but you must."

Unable to speak, incapable of uttering such a rush of words whirling hopelessly inside me, I can only nod once more. She reaches for my hand, and I try to move my fingers the tiniest bit so that she can feel their pressure. She leans over my hand, kisses it, and is gone.

THIS WOULD BE a good time to state the first of the principles I learned during this voyage: You must speak to those who are ill. Do not listen to the technicians and the scientists, the voices of authority and competence, the experts whose knowledge does not extend to the emotions and whose rationality limits their approach to life. Do not listen to those who tell you that the patient, even when co-matose—even dying, even dead!—does not hear you. You must speak to those who are considered beyond the reach of words, because words, in fact, get through. They need only be words of love.

Time Cannot Be Measured

FRANÇOISE DID MORE THAN lavish words of love on me. She repeated what the doctors had already come to tell me again and again the first time I woke up, and the second time, and the third—what the nurses had confirmed when I questioned them with the little plastic tablet and felt-tip pen.

"We haven't identified your illness yet. Blood and sputum samples have been taken and sent to Pathology. We're working on it. Once we know what we're dealing with, we'll be able to give you medication that should bring you some relief and reduce the edema. If we can do this, if the inflammation subsides, perhaps we can extubate you in a week or so."

I realized that, in the meantime, I'd have to spend at least seven or eight more days—and nights—attached to the bed, the IV, the respirator, racked with coughing fits, trembling with fever, swept along helplessly by the passage of immeasurable time. I would have to hang on for at least a week, day and night, and I would have to find a way to count those days and nights. If I could keep track of them, if I managed, like a prisoner scratching lines on a wall, to calculate the approaching moment of my deliverance, perhaps things would be easier for me. When you are heavily medicated and in severe pain, your notion of time is shattered. A vision may last a few seconds; you think it went on for an hour, or all day long. You cannot measure time anymore.

So I feel I must invent an idea of time for myself, find a way to track it: counting the nurses' work shifts, noticing everything that changes. Daylight, artificial light. The morning bustle of the ICU, the silence at night. The noises of my neighbor, Mr. Picolino, and his machine; his alarm is more frightening than mine—it sounds even more like an air-raid siren, a warning of panic aboard. Perhaps all this would help me define time. All this, as well as experiences and visits like the one I had just had: my first glimpse of my wife's face, the face of love. But I saw more than love in that face. I saw fear.

The Second Inner Voice

I SAW FEAR, because I was able to read that face I know so well. My wife's visit has left me exhausted, as if I've been doing some kind of hard physical exercise, some superhuman labor lasting for hours, like lifting tons of lead beneath a broiling sun. It's nighttime. I see Françoise's face again and think, "She must be very scared. I frightened her."

A surprising and disturbing thing now happens. Until this moment, whenever I've talked to myself, I've heard only one voice. This was simple and natural, and how it has been since earliest childhood: a single, inner voice. But a second voice now comes along to counter my familiar inner voice. The second voice is nothing like the first one.

"Well," says the newcomer, "if you frightened her, it's because you might be dying."

"Perhaps," I reply.

It's at the moment when this dialogue between Me and Me begins that I embark on a new stage of my journey. From now on, two voices will constantly overlap each other, like waves meeting in the middle of a stormy sea. These two voices are both mine, they are each a part of me, but they will clash in a duel that I alone will fight and witness. The voice of the temptation of death. The voice of the fight for life.

Children Must Learn to Laugh at Their Parents

IT'S LATE. I am so afraid of the night that after the nurse had taken care of me and was about to turn off the light before leaving, I became so agitated that she realized I wanted her to leave the light on in the room, which she did. Then she left. Now I'm alone and afraid. Afraid of everything. I'm already in physical pain, and when a vast, full-scale panic grips me, these two negative forces let despair rush in. The voice of the temptation of death speaks up again. "After all," it insists, "perhaps you're dying."

This time, my other voice—my usual voice, if I may call it that—is unable to reply. It's a defeat, a capitulation, the admission of an obvious fact. If my first voice, the familiar, normal one, has not been able to answer the second, new voice, it's because something else has taken hold of me along with my illness. The new voice continues. It's a rather pleasant voice, calm and courteous. Slightly condescending, a touch professorial, patronizing, avuncular.

"Well, yes," it murmurs. "After all," it purrs, "perhaps that's how it is. Oh, of course you hadn't expected this. You thought you had many more years left, lots of time ahead of you, but what can you do? Even if it's not what you planned, it's happening. Perhaps you'll be the first of the four brothers in your family to go. And yet you weren't the eldest, or even the second son, but nothing and nobody ever said that one leaves life in the order in which one entered it. Nothing! There's no law, it's not written anywhere. You'll just have to accept it. You'll be the first to rejoin your father."

The new voice has stopped speaking. Its words haunt me; they're all I hear now, echoing and tumbling around in my mouth and chest to the twelve-cycles-per-minute rhythm of the respirator. These words have become the sound of the machine, they are inseparable from my pain. And now I see that my visitors have returned.

HERE THEY ARE in the room. It's no longer as dark as it was before, surprisingly. Is it morning already? My guests are standing in a line along the wall, where the nurses usually post their care plans and consult their shift reports.

The visitors are standing motionless in a single row, wearing their usual clothes, smiling quietly. I wonder how they managed to slip into the room without my noticing. I probably closed my eyes and took one of those sudden plunges—impossible to time—into the fathomless depths of a semicoma. Why are these people here, not wearing the visitor's obligatory face mask, gloves, and gown, and without the authorization of the head nurse? Well, it isn't important. They are lined up nicely, looking at me with what I have already tried to describe as an attitude of boundless and patient indulgence. As if to say, "He doesn't seem in a hurry to come. He hasn't yet grasped that he doesn't have much of a choice. But it won't take long, he's a reasonable fellow, he'll join us eventually. Let's give him a little more time."

Enough time, perhaps, to identify them.

It isn't difficult. I recognize each of them instantly, since I know them by heart: the dead of my life. There's Valdo, who killed himself in Paris. In one of my novels, he died at twenty, dramatically, at the wheel of a car. In real life, he hanged himself when he was around fifty. There's my friend the director, Jean-Pierre, who died in my arms in a restaurant in the middle of a meal, from a ruptured aneurysm. How hard it had been for me to accept the loss of this friend, who was my mentor in the film world. Did I ever manage to fill the empty place he left in my life? There's May, who committed suicide in Maryland. There's Jean-François, murdered in Algiers. There's my father, who died in his bed, in Nice, with me, my mother, and one of my brothers at his side. There's Alice, she killed herself, too, in New York, on her fortieth birthday. She couldn't bear the thought of middle age. Or the ravages of drugs and loneliness. There's Dick, who died in a car crash in Mississippi. There's Boby, who died in a hospital in Besançon. Smiling, courageous, patient until the end, the very incarnation of love to his daughters—to his daughter, my wife. There are still more, among them a young girl and a bald, chubby little man. There must be a dozen of them, but since the new, inner voice specifically mentioned my father ("You'll be the first to rejoin your father"), he is the one I look at now.

HE IS WEARING his famous house jacket, a mid-thigh–length garment cut from the same material as a dressing gown, with red and green checks, ample pockets, and a wide belt. He always wore this jacket when he worked in his office. And if I say it was famous, that's because my brothers and I laughed at it behind my father's back. We admired and feared him, and would have found it impossible, in his presence or our mother's, to crack a single joke at his expense. But children must learn how to laugh at their parents. This slow debunking process, which begins at an early age, is something children cannot resist and parents must accept. Driven by the need to diminish the overwhelming image of the Father, we sought out the slightest detail that could provide comic relief from the monumental gravity of such a solemn and serious man. The house jacket belonged to the repertoire. It was so funny to imagine that he'd cut the bottom off a bathrobe to save money. That he looked like an English gentleman farmer. That all he needed was a pair of slippers made from the same fabric, and why not a nightcap, too? Did he sleep in the jacket? Take it on trips? That house jacket was so silly, old-fashioned, ancient, stuffy, and prim! We'd collapse in gales of delicious laughter at the simple mention of it. The Jacket.

At this particular moment, though, the house jacket no longer makes me laugh. Instead it's my father who is grinning at me from across the room. His usually severe expression has given way to an engaging smile. He is saying something. Still standing motionless against the wall of the hospital room, he is repeating, for the fifth or sixth time, "Come on. What are you waiting for?"

The Curious Man

WHY IS THE ONLY memory evoked by my father's presence in this room an image of mockery? Papa and his house jacket! Doesn't anything else come back to me besides this trivial recollection of childish laughter? Laughter from the 1940s, from nothing, from innocence, and golden days in the big garden filled with the rustle of poplar leaves stirring in the wind from the Tescou Valley, and the Tarn River . . . What levity, what superficiality, what a fleeting, powdery sensation. Nothing . . . A butterfly's wing, crumbling to dust at the touch of the past.

"Come," he says to me.

Yet I remain silent, motionless, unwilling to respond to his invitation. How can that be? My father, who loved me so, and whom I so loved, stands before me in flesh and blood. He really is there. I haven't seen him in ten years, since he lay on his deathbed in Nice and my mother closed his eyes, murmuring over and over again, "my dearest, my darling." He's talking to me, smiling at me, and I'm refusing to answer him? I hear some-one tell me, "Don't go over there."

It's my usual voice, the normal one, speaking up at last. Not the complacent, condescending new voice that has been telling me it's all over, the jig is up. No, it's the other one, the familiar Me, my life. The voice of life, making itself heard.

"Look at them," it tells me. "They're poking fun at you. You can see they're laughing at you."

Actually, I do have a vague feeling that they're sneering at me, all those masklike faces that seem so friendly. I begin to distrust them. Why should I go join them? Then I hear the voice of death.

"Don't be ridiculous. If they're smiling at you, it's because they love you and want to welcome you. All they're asking is that you stop struggling in a useless battle that's already lost. Look at those smiles: do you see anything mean and scornful in them, anything that displeases you?"

It's true that there's nothing displeasing about that long line of patient men and women who have so kindly come to see me at what is, after all, an inconvenient time in this ICU, where visits aren't usu-ally allowed. My guests are not upsetting in any way. May is as lovely as ever, and my friend the director—with his white hat and black Ray•Bans hiding those big eyes (he never liked their color)—is still just as fascinating.

May: as lovely as ever . . . Her amber eyes light up her black face. She's wearing a pale dress with a fitted waist and buttons down the front. Her lips seem to offer that same forbidden gift, that same sa-vor of wine and fruit as when I used to kiss her, timidly, madly, in the back seat of a car borrowed from a student who had more money than I did.

HE HAD NEVER forgotten May.

During his second year in America, to relieve the boredom that had begun to dog him on the pretty, sleepy little campus in Virgina, and to satisfy his curiosity, he had spent some time trying to track her down in the "Negro" part of town. He was more experienced now, a bit better at lying, faking, even bribing, so he had finally dug up some information. May was no longer living with her family and had gone to Maryland. At that point, deciding it was really over, he had resolved not to think about her anymore and to go out only with coeds. But he had never forgotten that secret love and the young woman who had revealed to him the power of sensuality. Who had made him come with pleasure, a different pleasure than the one his own hands had brought him until then, during his adolescence.

Eight or ten years later, he had found himself in Baltimore dur-ing his endless search for the truth about John F. Kennedy's death. He must have devoted about three years of his journalistic career to that story. He knew everything about it—in other words, nothing. The more you look, the less you understand. He knew it all by heart: the map of the city, the streets, the schedules, the names. He had become a walking encyclopedia of data on November 22, 1963, in

Dallas. At the time, he had belonged to a network of scholars, librarians, reporters, researchers, detectives, criminologists, and politicians, most of them American, who constantly exchanged theories and leads, news and revelations. One particular tip had taken him to Baltimore.

"If you want to meet Santos," his informant had told him, "go to the hotel and wait until he gets in touch with you. Don't leave the hotel."

He had waited for two days. The wait had strung him out. He knew he was in the city where May had gone. Was she still there? He began to comb the phone books with listings for Baltimore and its suburbs, turning up a dozen people with the same family name as May's. He had dialed the numbers, compulsively, one after the other.

"Hello, may I please speak to May?" His voice was low, conspiratorial.

"There's no May here, you've got the wrong number."

On the eighth try, he thought he recognized her southern accent, the hoarse, raspy voice that could turn teasing and intimate, but bitter, too.

"Who's this?" the voice said. "Who wants to speak to May?"

Just the sound of the voice had wound him up tight. He'd felt seized once again by the same desire, the same hunger that used to overwhelm him when he was eighteen, during their brief encounters in the back seat of the Buick.

"Who is this?" the voice repeated.

"A friend of hers," he answered, "from a while back."

He was trying to be cautious and discreet. Was she living alone, he wondered? Was there a man around? Children, relatives? Silence at the other end of the line.

"May?" he said. "Hello?"

She spoke slowly, quietly.

"Who are you?" she whispered.

He found her words loaded with all sorts of meanings: astonishment, disbelief, but a slight tone of invitation as well, and a hint of something mean, almost rude. And then he realized he was mistaken. He had thought he recognized the voice of his lost love because he had hoped to find her again, but now something about the way the voice had said "Who are you?" was telling him he was wrong. Suddenly, the girl had laughed on the phone. A short, sad little laugh. The rush of sexual desire melted away.

"You want May," the girl said, "but she's not here anymore. I'm a cousin. May's gone. She took her own life last year, if you really want to know."

She took her own life. We use amazing expressions to avoid saying the words that frighten us the most, and rather than say "She killed herself," or "She's dead," we prefer this sibylline formula: she took her own life.

He had mumbled apologies, incapable of asking a single question. He'd hung up. He found himself alone in a strange hotel room, overcome with anxiety and an insatiable curiosity. Why did she do it? What had she become? The sour feeling of his mistake, of the deception of that voice in the night, and the paranoia in the closeness of that room, would stay with him for a long time, well after he had left Baltimore.

Thereafter the assassination of the president and the suicide of his first love would remain linked in his mind. Santos did finally call, owning up to his statement, a few months before Dallas, "Kennedy's a stone in my shoe." But that solved nothing.

HE HAD A PERSONAL conviction about Dallas.

Since he liked to travel, and since he was then a great reader of detective stories, he decided that trying to determine the truth of the assassination would allow him to play a role in a real-life thriller. He had been willing to pretend, to deceive, because he loved to chase scoops, ferret out secrets, and unearth the tiny fragments of a puzzle that would prove impossible to put together. Like all the other investigators, he had agreed to play along with the theory that there hadn't been one plot, but many. And yet, whenever he seriously studied his material and searched his memory, the firm conviction resurfaced. At the time, he was just about the only one who thought along those lines. It was almost a blasphemy, but he didn't say it out loud or write it down. All he had to do was think back to Lee Harvey Oswald's twisted smile in the fifth-floor hallway of the Dallas police station, a grimace he had personally observed from not more than a yard away—all he had to do was think about that smile and his belief was confirmed.

After countless long nights haunted by the mournful sirens of boats and the wail of patrol cars, and early mornings filled with the cries of seagulls, and the cheerful cacophony of the harbor, his only memory of Baltimore remained the news about May, the death of the young black woman he had loved when he was still raw and inexperienced. And this was all that mattered.

"She took her own life."

SO, NOW, May is here before me, in the ICU room, among the other visitors. May, who seems frail yet tough, with her arms crossed on her chest. She's smiling, too, but it's not the same smile as my father's. There's no trace left of that provocative amusement I used to see in her eyes when we'd meet secretly in the Buick, during that chilly, southern winter in Virginia forty years ago, when we loved talking as much as making love, and talking some more, and making love again, when the South was southern—in other words, deadly for whoever dared break the rules that kept the races apart. Today, in May's smile, I no longer see anything but indulgence, almost forgiveness. I tell myself that if she has come to visit me, it's so that I can finally receive an answer to the question I hadn't dared ask her so-called cousin one evening in Baltimore.

"May, tell me, why did you take your own life?"

But she disappears from view while my gaze shifts to a third visitor.

"Forget those people," says my familiar voice. "Drop them. Let them go. Don't look at them anymore. Forget death. Try your hardest to look at a different spot in the room. Look away, you fucking idiot, or you're not going to make it. Don't let yourself be sucked in by them. Look away!"

I try. It seems tremendously difficult. I manage to tear my eyes away from the row of people along the wall and find a place in the room where there are no visitors. And into this empty space pour wave after wave of blue Colorado firs. I'm flooded with blue.

In these endless billows of blue, green, yellow, and black, I see the purity that so attracted me when I was eighteen and knew nothing of life. Lying on the rock, with the wind whipping through my clothes and all down my body, I could barely turn my head to find out if my friends, stretched out with me on the Notch itself, were as enthralled as I was by this spectacle. What was strange was that we didn't talk about it very much when we got back to camp later on. When we gathered around the stove in our tent, we made only a few comments about our climb to the Notch and the sights along the way. Perhaps we didn't have the words to talk about what we had seen. My companions were innocent, as was I—innocent about life.

Popa, Where's Popa?

WHEN PEOPLE CLAIM that you see your whole life pass before your eyes during an accident, a drowning, an operation, or some other close call with death, you should ask them to be more specific, or more straightforward. Of course, since all experience is by definition unique, what these people say is perhaps true. But I don't believe it. I no longer believe it.

I believe—because I know—that you see your own life, yes, but you don't see it "pass before your eyes" like a chronological series of events. You see only fragments, tatters, a jumble of life. It's chaos, a charivari, a maelstrom, a kaleidoscope in furious motion with no hand to steady the image. Everything is shattered, exploded, pulverized, as though you were in a cauldron or a tube turning in all directions, shaking up bits of debris from life. Or from dreams. You're at the epicenter of a sort of earthquake. You are the earthquake. And what's astonishing is that the scattered scraps of life you see again aren't necessarily the most important ones.

A SHIMMER OF IMAGES. A shimmer of memory.

A small plane takes off from the airport in Amman. Dusty ocher sand; impassive, mustached faces. White buildings dwindling away as we gain altitude. The plane is full of rough characters dressed in fatigues, carrying weapons. Killers and mercenaries, deserters, double agents. A cargo of irregulars, of troublemakers. (I no longer remember how we wangled permission to get on board, but it was the last crate to leave for Beirut before the little king decided to put the entire Western press corps in quarantine. This was at the end of the fifties.) We run into heavy turbulence over the mountains between Jordan and Lebanon, and hit a huge air pocket. Stuff flies all over in the cabin as the plane takes a severe buffeting. It's like being on a roller coaster. Your heart and stomach do flipflops. Tough guys turn pale. Everyone's puking. You hear whimpering and mewing sounds, but there aren't any children or animals on board. The moans and groans are coming from the "men of war." Peculiar substances are running in rivulets down the center aisle. The sky is black. Have we been swallowed up by a sandstorm? A guy wearing a machine gun is on his knees, intoning prayers. Next to me I hear Pradas, the hard-bitten photographer who accompanies me everywhere, shouting, "The devil's asshole! We're going to see the devil's asshole!"

He seems excited at the prospect. And the plane seems about to go into a spin. Nauseated, I watch as my bag sails by, with all my papers and notebooks. Now we're looping. There's deafening pressure in our ears. And then, suddenly, all is brightness and calm, the plane is flying smoothly again, and we're already heading in for a landing. The men in the cabin are a pathetic sight, wiping away vomit with their red-and-white-checked kaffiyehs. Pradas looks haggard.

"We didn't see it," he says regretfully. "We came close, but we didn't see it."

Outside is Beirut: fresh air. As our feet touch the ground, it occurs to me that I didn't think about death at all, not even for a second. I'm twenty-one years old. It never touched me. It was too soon. It wasn't for me.

A SHIMMERING of images and memories.

The kindness in the eyes of the priest, whom I've finally run to ground outside a chapel in Buenos Aires. His look of kindly amusement when I tell him that I've come ten thousand kilometers to hear him tell me how he saved twenty lives when a ferry boat sank in the freezing waters of the Mar del Plata. The priest refuses to talk about his heroism and says simply, "I wasn't afraid, I was waiting to be saved, waiting for God to take my hand again."

THE BROTHERS on their bikes, pedaling along the main street to school. Everything is joyous, peaceful, limpid, and clear. All of childhood is in the music of those wire wheels, which sing louder as the slope increases . . .

THE SCATHING LAUGHTER of the druggies in California, in the late sixties, out in the hills of Topanga Canyon at night; their eyes that gleamed orange in the firelight, their messy hair, their arrogant and absolutely meaningless theological babblings—and their determination that I should share their world view, which forced me to flee by crawling alongside a swimming pool only to wind up on my hands and knees in the thorny brush at the edge of a desert. I must have looked really scary, because I walked for eight hours that night before a car deigned to stop and give me a lift. I felt like a dog.

CHRISTMAS IN the big house, and Mama's voice singing, "Born Is Jesus the Infant King."

The Alfa Romeo turns over three times on a mountain road near the Swiss border with Italy. I'm the only one in the car, from which I emerge without a scratch. Some locals stare at me, aghast.

"You almost bought it with that one!"

Mortar fire over the Casbah. Women with their throats cut in the Hydra neighborhood. The capricious fury of a movie star punching and kicking a set to pieces; he turns to me and the crew, who haven't moved a muscle, and shouts, "Nobody gets close-ups but me!"

The bare feet of children out in the sunshine, crushing muscat grapes in vats at harvest time, in the south of France. Trains I tried to catch at a run; a pillow I can't seem to find anywhere; my unspeakable fear after an anonymous phone call in a Dallas hotel, with a Texan voice at the other end of the line: "Get out of town and don't come back"; a flight of black crows over the gardens of the psychiatric hospital in Vienna.

A memory of the Pyrenees. A cold lake, serene and icy blue. A boat. I'm eight years old. I had chest problems, so I was sent there to build up my strength. Children as sickly as I was lived in a chalet on the edge of a lake. I hear the strains of an old song.

And then I wonder, back in my hospital room in the ICU, if all that I'm living through—or rather, dying through—isn't linked to that episode of my childhood. I wonder if it all began back there.

Everything shimmers.

The earthquake continues, since I jump from my early years to those of my own children. I hear my little son Jean, in Sierra Leone, outside the straw hut where I'm writing. He's seen a big lizard run across the path and he shouts, "Popa, where's Popa?"

For a few moments, his funny exclamation rolls around in my head, POPAWARESPOPA, and I see his sister Clarisse's little hands playing patty-cake with his. This time, they're somewhere else, in Kenya, sitting in the scrub next to a runway of dirt and grass, waiting for a prop plane. They're playing nonsense games with their own private songs.

> Pépito, he's the captain
> The captain of the boat,
> Pépito, he's the captain,
> The captain of the ship.

And I turn around to see their mother's face beaming fondly, her hazel eyes sparkling beneath her khaki bush hat. She's smiling.

Everything shimmers.

THE SHIMMERING of memory is not necessarily painful. Suffering is always there, of course: bodily suffering. But I'll spare you that tale of woe. You cannot tell anyone about pain. In any case, I feel that I have neither the talent nor the inclination for it. It's horribly repetitious, pain. Horribly the same. It doesn't stop, that's all, and that's all you need to say. It never lets up, in your chest, your throat, your entire body, and you're furious with the whole world, the nurses, the tubes and the respirator, your own weakness, because you're suffering so much, but you become so familiar with the pain that in the end, you accept it. You accept everything, even the unacceptable. You must. You have no choice. It seems—I think it was Dostoyevsky who said so—that the best definition of man is this: "A creature who gets used to everything." So am I a man, since I'm getting used to this pain?

Over and over, I say to myself, "The capital of pain." Is it the title of a poem, of a novel? It doesn't matter, the image suits me, it's appropriate: my address is the capital of Pain, on Bedridden Boulevard, Respirator Street, Semicomatose Alley, Blocked Larynx Square, in the Unknown and Unidentified Bacteria Wing, on the IV floor, in the Intensive Care Room. In the neighborhood of despair.

If I do bear the pain, it's because—contrary to what I think—the pain is not always relentless. The medication they give me certainly provides short stretches of relief, beaching me in a quasi-coma, slipping me into an ersatz slumber. Into a different state. Is it in this state that I see my carpet of blue again? Is it at this stage that the bits and pieces of my life rattle around chaotically, in their random earthquake? Some of them shoot quickly by, like meteors; others return regularly, hauntingly. That's how it is with these images that chase all the others away: the Eagle's Notch, the Uncompahgre forest.

The forest is beautiful, like the sea, like silk; I'm drawn to it, submerged in it, and I forget the people lined up along the wall, I forget the respirator, the breathing and intravenous tubes, and I no longer feel the same, piercing need to press the call button for the nurse. I stop worrying about the pulse oximeter, that little cap of grooved rubber, ringed with metal, that's attached to the tip of my left index finger, where it constantly measures the percentage of oxygen in my blood.

The oximeter plays a vital role, however, in what I manage to see of my body, which just lies there, enfeebled, stretched out flat on the bed. At the end of my finger, the oximeter gives off a faint orange glow. I quickly figure out that it's a comforting object, and if I had the strength to make the comparison, it would remind me of E.T.'s gleaming fingertip. When the nurse's aides take care of me, turning me over, handling this body that no longer has either muscles or weight (how many pounds have I lost?), I can easily see how important the oximeter is from the way they make sure it isn't off my finger for very long. I've noticed that the first thing they do after they've finished bathing me is to quickly reattach the oximeter to my fingertip. And because they do this, I've understood that I need it there, and so I like it there. As long as I can feel the little rubber sheath on my finger, I can tell myself that all is not lost.

Well, now that my eyes, head, and even the room have been flooded with blue, the oximeter doesn't matter anymore. I've become one with those endless waves of fir trees. Right now, I'm lying on the Notch and it's cold, but that doesn't bother me. I don't know what my friends think, but I'm beginning to find the ocean of blue trees as seductive as the legend says they are. I tell myself that if I were to plunge into that sea, I'd simply cross over to the other side and discover something completely unknown to me.

But I was eighteen, and so were my friends, and we didn't leap into the void to crash onto the tops of the ponderosa pines below. We went back down to our camp without mentioning any temptations we might have felt. It's true that my companions weren't particularly loquacious. Pacheco, Branch, Donald, and the Swede were neither great intellectuals nor great talkers. But why now, today, in this room in the ICU, is the ocean of fir trees calling to me once more? What does it mean?

I have barely had time to contemplate the blue firs when the voice of death moves in on me again. Suddenly, the trees are gone, the row of people is gone. The visitors have left the room. Have they decided to go eat a bite in the cafeteria, then return to the ICU? The voice of death hastens to reply. It's still just as pleasant, just as helpful as ever, the voice of death.

"Don't worry. They promised they'd return to see you. They'll be back soon."

I hate that voice. I like mine so much better. Which one of these two voices at odds within me will win? The duel begins.

The Power of Laughter
and Poetry

IT'S NIGHT TIME AGAIN, and I'm still just as afraid. And I can feel myself growing weaker. The voice of death drones on and on.

"Let yourself go," it says. "The doctors haven't found anything, or else they'd have come to tell you. They're leaving you pretty much alone, don't you think? It's very quiet in the ICU this evening. No noise out in the hallway—except for poor Mr. Picolino's call bell. This must be your third or fourth night here. Your strength is ebbing. Do you really think you're going to be able to last until morning? Aren't you beginning to get tired of this?"

I can't get rid of the voice.

"Well," it continues, "here's Karen the Korean. In a moment she's going to hurt you again. When she changes the ties, hangs a new IV, takes your temperature, and worst of all, checks your blood gases—that horrible procedure! Her thumb's going to be rock hard, pressing on your artery. 'This will be a bit painful,' she'll warn you, in her shrill, vulgar voice. And then she'll hurt you. She doesn't want you to get better. Karen is too preoccupied with getting ahold of her father in Seoul. She wasted half her day phoning, trying to get through to wish him a happy Father's Day. She's getting along worse and worse with her mother's lover. They had another scene last night, before she came to work at the hospital. She told the whole story to her shift partner, the little nurse with the mean voice. It's going to be another night of hell with these two, don't you think?"

I need to find a weapon, something that will help me resist this warped voice of death. The only weapon I have is the one the voice itself uses: words. I need to go deep inside myself to look for the simplest words, the most obvious points, the most telling replies. So I talk to myself in my own voice, the voice of my life.

"Stop panicking, calm down. Get a grip and laugh at death. Sneer in its shitty face. It's not time yet, and you're not interested. Just say it. You tell death, 'Beat it! Fuck off!' Come on, are you going to let that punk get the better of you? You're not going to cave in, after all—you've been through worse than this!"

That's not true, I haven't been through anything worse than this. I wasn't ready for this. Who is? But I've found the right approach, and I tear into myself. I shake myself. I whip, scold, nag, and insult myself. I stick to the stern, arrogant attitude. I decide, in the end, to laugh at death. A nasty laugh, the way a bully laughs when he knows he's tougher than the jerk who's trying to beat him up. The way a soldier laughs at the front, in his trench, when the enemy's artillery has been pounding him for two hours straight. The landscape all around him has been reduced to shell craters and charred trees, but he's still hunkered down in the mud with his helmet on his head and his weapon in the crook of his arm, on his knees in the dust, the ashes, the smoke, and the deafening noise, and his mind is still clear, and he laughs. "Hang in there," he tells himself simply.

I'm not surprised to be falling back on such stock phrases. They're not really ideas, just words. Plain, everyday words. And then I'm not in a position to evaluate the originality of what I'm saying. My sophisticated friends would call me naive, disgustingly earnest, practically simple-minded. "What, no irony?" they'd say. "You sound like a moron!" But what friends are we talking about? Where are they? Not one of them is here to help me. I'm all alone. Alone in the world. So I go right on laughing.

"Just laugh," I keep telling myself. "You'll pull through. You're going to fuck death. You're going to screw it. There's that hard-rock band, Screw Your Mother. Well, you can Screw Your Death!

Cursing death makes me feel better. Using vulgar language is stimulating, it reinforces my hostility and a vision of my survival, it stops my body from giving up.

"You're gonna screw that bitch. You're gonna screw all those assholes. That cunt will shut up but good."

And I really pour on all this coarse stuff, to drown out that other voice, to keep from winding up helpless.

Now my every effort will be devoted to preventing that voice of death from coming back inside me, from cutting off my other voice.

I have to keep the voice of death out of my body, deny it any chance of slipping into my throat and making more of its insinuations. So a new reflex of self-defense will kick in, something else I've never experienced before, since I'm crossing unknown territory. I begin endlessly repeating a series of words and phrases, leaving not a fraction of a second of silence in my head. If I were able to coldly analyze what I'm doing, I would say that it's a bit like chanting a mantra.

In the first stage of self-control, the conscientious repetition of one or more sets of words can stop the flow of images battering the mind and pushing it into darkness. Without realizing it, I'm creating a ritual of repetitive formulas for myself that will help me stave off weakness and resignation. The temptation of the void, the spectacle of nothingness, the leap into the abyss. And you must never— I'm learning this as well—give the abyss more than forty seconds' advantage.

So everything turns up in my mantra, whatever is churned out by the absurd unconscious. And in my case, on this particular night, this produces a wealth of verses, bits of poems, scraps of text from long ago, tag ends of my modest personal culture, my interior baggage, dumped out every which way, like suitcases bursting open at a train wreck. Along with these fragments come proper names from I don't know where, and I have no idea why.

This proceeds in cycles, and I will go from one name repeated a hundred times to another, or from one bit of verse to another. For no reason. There is no reason, in fact, why the name of a man I've never met should suddenly pop up: Christophe de Ponfily. Why has this name appeared? I pronounce it in an almost musical fashion, chanting it over and over, pausing briefly between certain syllables: "Chris-tophe (I emphasize the *e*) de Ponfily."

There is no reason why this "Chris-tophe *e e e* de Ponfily" should protect me from the temptation of the abyss. But why should there be a reason? And furthermore, is there any reason why, after I have no idea how many hundred—or even thousand—Ponfilys, I should start in on the title of a book I've never read, a title I'm not even sure really exists, *La Volte des Vertugadins*? The same phenomenon takes over my inner voice and whatever remains of my faculties, the same mania for breaking up words and turning them into ritual chants, incantations: "La Vol-te-des-Ver-tugadins."

Again, this mantra runs through my head hundreds of times. Then my mind tires, drifting toward sentences rather than words; dozens and dozens of poetic extracts crowd into my thoughts, but I am unable to get beyond the second or third verse of any poem.

I think that if I had been able to sort through this hodgepodge of poetry, I'd have made some sense of it. First off, it all had to do with the passage of time. The fragments were steeped in melancholy and nostalgia. Also, what sprang most readily to mind was the verse I'd learned at an early age, as a schoolboy. So does this mean that when you're getting close to death, the first thing you remember is your childhood? And your youth? Does that explain the haunting memories of Colorado? And does it mean you're returning to your childish state?

Yes, I'm becoming more and more a child. I'm searching for my childhood—all the images of the past that have come rushing back to me prove this. And I'm reduced to childlike helplessness, like a baby in maternal care. My mamas are the nurses. I wait for them, the way a baby awaits his bottle. And just as he cries because he's hungry, afraid, or in pain, I cry in my own way, by pressing the call bell that sounds the alarm and summons help to my side.

I MIGHT HAVE despaired at remembering only the bare beginnings of a few poems, but I just laugh at all that and go on with my litanies, telling myself that this, too, will help me to hold on. And I laugh at myself as well.

"If they opened up your brain to try to discover who you are, this is all they'd find to say: 'He was a man whose entire stock of knowledge consisted of random verses from certain poems of French literature, the tritest lines, the easiest to remember. He was incapable of going further. That's what he was.'"

Another question slips into my delirium, my mantra. It's not the voice of death questioning me, the voice I've managed to stifle thanks to my poems. I haven't heard from that voice for a while now. But the question seems like one it would ask.

"What would you like people to say about you, if you aren't destined to make it back?"

I don't answer. Perhaps I tell myself, just once, "I'd like them to say, 'He was a decent human being.'"

So then: your family, the children, your love for your wife, your passion for books and films, the excitement of creative work, success and failure, the crowing of vanity, stardust, what goes nowadays by the fancy label of "communication," the influence you fondly thought you had over certain men and women, your experience as a film director, your mentors and disciples, your role as a company executive, the fame you won or lost and the illusion of having gained something from it . . . So then: nothing of this should matter if you were to go? All you want is that people would be able to say, "He was a decent human being"? But if this is what's on your mind, it's probably because you don't consider yourself that decent.

The Liar with the Coconuts

WHAT EXACTLY IS A "decent human being"? An expression not often heard anymore today. It's too old-fashioned, from his father's time.

He remembered one autumn day in Paris, on what were called the Grand Boulevards. His father—wearing that everlasting hat, gazing calmly and imperiously through the heavy frames of his glasses—had held his hand as they walked along. And fresh from the provinces, still wet behind the ears, the child had looked around in utter astonishment.

They were strolling together, father and son. It was a present, a treat, since the father considered the simple spectacle of the crowd of hurrying passersby to be ample reward for the first good grades from school, a big school with a vast playground and knowing, streetwise students quick to make fun of the little "country boy" with the accent. As the grades had been "acceptable" (an intentionally modest evaluation by his father, who believed one should not overwhelm a child with praise—or criticism, either), a reward had been announced: "Tomorrow I'll take you out on the Grand Boulevards."

They'd walked to the Carrefour Haussmann, stopping to enjoy an iced coffee with whipped cream, while standing up at a high, round table in a new kind of establishment: a Maison du Café . The little boy had observed mustaches, red hair, skinny people, rich people, coquettes and demure young things, men in suits—and women, too. After the vast provincial garden of his childhood, he was so unused to crowds that this motley vision of humanity intrigued him. He tried to see beneath the surface, to see behind these faces. He felt that some of them were playing a role, while others were not. Had the father sensed, perhaps, his son's silent perplexity? "Come," he said, leaning down to the child. "I'm going to show you what a liar looks like."

Then they'd lingered on that stretch of boulevard near the entrance to the metro, where the illegal street vendors were lined up. Some hawked kitchen wares, cakes of soap, pralines, with everything set out on planks laid across two sawhorses. Others, less fortunate, had only a large umbrella set upside down on the asphalt in which to display their merchandise. That way they could quickly shut up shop if an overzealous policeman should demand to see permits they clearly did not possess.

"Take a good look," said the boy's father. "There is a liar. There is a representation of life."

Three vendors were selling the same thing: wretched pieces of coconut cut into triangles. There was hardly anybody in front of the first two. Everyone was clustered around the third man. Yet he was offering exactly what the other two were selling.

The third vendor had lots of black hair, a bull neck, thick lips, and eyebrows that were constantly in motion on a broad, sensual face. He spoke rapidly and well, smiling as he talked, and never seemed to need to catch his breath. His hands were squarish, with strong, blunt fingers, and he would shoot his cuffs to fiddle with the buttons at his sleeves—a gesture that the little boy had never seen before and would later recognize, in manhood, as an infallible sign of vulgarity, of cocksureness, of cheeky, bantering humor, and an unshakable sense of superiority over all rivals. This artist held forth in an irresistible Parisian accent, oily and smug, laid on with a gusto that was repellent, of course, yet inevitably seductive. The man had the gift of gab and a raffish charm. He was unstoppable, and no one on the boulevard even considered trying. His sales pitch rose and fell, drowning out those of the other two vendors.

"Come closer, closer ladies and gentlemen. If you want to know why my coconut is better than that of my colleagues nearby, I'll tell you. Would you like me to tell you why my coconut is better? Well, I'm going to tell you, it's a revelation—because it's the best, that's why! There are some who will tell you they sell excellent coconut, delicious coconut, authentic coconut, true African coconut from our wonderful colonies, from our wonderful Negroes. There are some who will tell you they sell superb coconut at a most reasonable price and I wouldn't contradict them. Not at all. I would never think of wronging these nice fellows who've made the mistake of setting up shop on my territory. I wish them no harm, and I'm sure they're right, but neither of them has dared or will dare to tell you that their coconut is the best of the lot and I'm the only one who can promise you that and I do promise you that: if you buy it, you'll see that my coconut is better than all others. Do you want to know why it's better? I'm going to tell you without further ado: quite simply because it's the best. My coconut, ten centimes a slice, is the best coconut, because it's the best."

The father had taken the little boy's hand in his own once again and had led him away from the street vendor, who continued his endless spiel.

"You understand quickly when someone is lying. The patter is always attractive, but you understand, because it's always the same patter. And in the end you realize that the liar himself believes it. This is the most dangerous kind of liar. So you see, this man is not a decent man."

The father's words are from a long time ago. As I lie here, they resurface in a mind possessed by illness, haunted by death. Am I a liar myself? Have I lied a lot in my life? Have I always acted in good faith? And more important, have I always been worthy of what I should have wanted to be, of what I would have liked my father and mother, and those I love, to think of me? Have I hurt many people? Have I given so little?

These questions come and go rapidly. I have neither the strength nor the time to dwell on them. But they return me to that childish state I spoke of a moment ago: the baby waiting for its bottle. I push the call button to bring the "mamas," the nurses, to my side.

Because, like all babies, I have nightmares.

And Now, Darkness

I THOUGHT I HAD SILENCED the second voice and won a kind of battle, thanks to my word games and scattered poems. But just when I thought I might have earned some sort of respite, a new door opened onto darkness. Here are things that are simply unfathomable.

The Top-Men and the Black Tunnel

I TRY TO REST. Karen the Korean is in the room, busy with her care plans, checking her orders. She turns her back to me. The machine and I are "working" more or less in harmony. I think I'll finally be able to sleep a bit. Yet I've hardly closed my eyes when I see soft, melting, orangey-yellowish things appear, hanging from the ceiling overhead. They're about to engulf me.

I find myself in a room decorated like those American hotel rooms that turned up everywhere in the mid-seventies, when the entire world began to resemble a California-Florida motel bedroom, with artificial plants, fake flames in the fireplace, thick carpet in fluorescent colors, fancy ornamentation on the walls and doors, moldings and rococo stuff all over. The acme of bad taste, of the standardization of vulgarity. Everything is planned so that this décor and this ambience will provide the hotel guest with a holiday feeling of escape, relaxation, and relief from stress. In my case, the décor will undergo some remodeling.

Objects, furniture, and paintings will begin to soften and change into a kind of orangey dough that creeps inexorably in my direction, as though to suffocate and bury me. Like stalactites of taffy sagging down from a vault to wrap themselves around me. It's threatening, terrifying, because I'm lying paralyzed on my bed and cannot escape. At the same time, some funny little creatures appear.

Actually, they really are funny at first. They're short, roly-poly men, like tops, without waists or hips. There is a whole crowd of them, and they're in a jovial mood. They're wearing British cricket caps—which give them an elegant and distinguished air, on the whole—but also ugly, baggy pants in rainbow checks with wide suspenders, circus-clown style. They've got clown mugs, besides: bulbous red noses, silly ears. They're jolly—that's the only precise description I can give—and they wriggle on their two short, fat legs as though about to perform a kind of round dance. I hear carnival music: zim boom boom. Drums and cymbals, muted trumpets, and a plaintive melody from what sounds like a dance-hall piano. The rhythm reminds me of fairground or parade music, in a majorette style but with tropical accents as well, a Caribbean or Afro-Cuban sound. A Junkanoo festival. RAT-TA-TAM—BOOM-BOOM—ZINGA-ZINGA-BOOM. It's stupid and stupefying, but after a moment or so, it's scary.

The little men keep laughing at me. They seem to find me irresistibly amusing. What's happening to me is all a big joke to them. As if to emphasize that they just couldn't care less, they doff their caps to me, then plop them back on their Humpty-Dumpty heads. Now a beach appears all around them, with umbrellas, striped rubber rafts, wooden piers with gaudy flags—like a seaside resort of the 1920s. The beach is thronged with these little fellows, who make strange tourists and even stranger entertainers. And there's still the deafening confusion of that jangling carnival music—I can't figure out where it's coming from or why it's here. Until now, everything I've seen or heard in my head had some connection to my life, my lives, my memory, and past experiences. But this landscape, this music, these clowns in their cricket caps aren't connected to anything. They have nothing to do with me! It makes no sense. But it's frightening, because the apparition of these top-men coincides with the slow and inexorable flow of orange lava closing in on me, dropping from the walls and ceiling. It's a double threat: this creeping ooze and these weird guys bouncing around, patting their bellies.

Who are these cackling dwarfs? What do they want from me? They're called Death. Their strained hilarity begins to seem threatening. They're not laughing at all anymore. They're coming closer. Their faces and bodies have decomposed; they've turned into monsters, mixing themselves up with one another like that orange lava flow in a kind of grotesque, nightmarish, copulative frenzy. They're naked. I'm going crazy. My mind is one long silent scream.

Then, with a desperate effort, I open my eyes. I think that if I can keep my eyes open, the top-men will go away. Karen the Korean isn't here. I study my surroundings and recognize the hallway of the ICU on my left, the dim light over the nurses' work counter on my right, the oximeter on my fingertip. I can feel the IV in my left forearm, the tubes, the respirator. Everything is here. If you keep your eyes open, I tell myself, the monsters won't come back. Hang on! And I begin to wonder.

Why must I be attacked like this? Is this what death is? Your body suffers, they tie you down and stick tubes in your throat, you get weaker and feel yourself going, but not only that, you go crazy as well? This is death? It's losing your mind, going insane? So when I plunge into the black tunnel opening up in front of me, I'll go completely out of my mind? And die demented?

Because there is a gaping, sooty tunnel. Have I closed my eyes again, or did the tunnel just appear before me in the middle of the wall in this ICU room? It seems dark and endless, and I fall into it. I see myself fall in. I slip and slide and can't hold on to anything, I'm in free fall, into darkness. Everything is black and there's nothing but this blackness and this black void and I just keep falling, in utter terror, with the realization that my life has been nothing but a useless black comedy applauded by cretins who will devour me to the accompaniment of calypso music.

BLACK. It doesn't surprise me at all to be plummeting through that color, because it's the color of my illness. I said earlier that pain cannot be described. Now, however, I must try to give some idea of the pain: it's like a black fire in the chest. It's devastating. It's thick and it makes noise, an inhuman sound that doesn't belong to the land of the living. I've been told that rounding Cape Horn is like that: you're on an ocean that explodes with each wave, up to the crest, then down into the trough, the black hole. You lose track of the horizon, lose any sense of balance and direction, and you can't imagine how it all will end.

The sound of the waves is the respirator. The blackness is the fluid that has invaded my lungs and swollen my larynx, and it's into this roaring blackness that I fall, tumbling toward my tomb. I tumble into death. Death is opening its door to me.

But I'm still able to talk to myself, and as I fall, I hear myself say, "If you open your eyes again, you'll come back. That's all it would take to bring you out of the tunnel. Slam on the brakes, shift into reverse, don't give up! Hang on!"

Am I saved? I feel as though I were coming back. Once again, Cape Horn: they also say that leaving that hell of howling winds seems like salvation, rescue, deliverance. I'm not out of it yet, but I feel that I'm hanging on and that I'm coming back. And if I am hanging on, it's because something has saved me. I think I know what has saved me—and can save me.

I know that I cannot die insane, because I know that I am not insane. Someone once wrote that madness was "when one is no longer capable of either work or love." I can't work anymore, that's obvious. Perhaps I will no longer be able to write books, direct films, or manage a radio station, cherishing the staff, listening to them, trusting them, and hoping they will return this trust. I understand all that, since I can barely move and breathe, since I'm an invalid, a frail thing strapped to a bed, tethered to life by a machine that never stops going BOOM-BOOM-RAT-TA-TAM and Beeeep! Beeeep! whenever it decides I've fallen out of sync with it. A shitty machine—I hate it and can't manage to understand that I can't live without it. No longer able to work, true enough! But love? I can still love.

That I can't love anymore and am therefore insane is a lie. I want to love and I do love. During my fall in the black tunnel, that, I believe, is what halted my plunge toward death. That is what held me back.

18

A Few Brief Words from the Log

EIGHTEEN MONTHS LATER, thanks to the friendship of those who had cared for and healed me, I was able to read a few lines in the ICU nurses' log. To ensure the authenticity of this book, I tried to find out how my descent into the tunnel and my vision of all those creatures and things had been reported by the nurses taking care of me. That endless fall into a black void, those nights of fear and struggle, nights I remember as those of the long, dark voyage, the great crossing—how were they written up by a professional and objective observer?

There were only a few words.

"Patient awake all night," said the ICU nurses' log. "Unable to sleep in spite of 15 drops of Tercian."

The following night: "Very anxious. Reassure him."

The young woman had added three plus signs after "Reassure him," as a sign to the nurse on the next shift.

The following night, one of them had written, "Patient extremely upset. Sometimes panicky. Tires easily."

So few words . . .

It was in the course of these three nights that I had my first near-death experience. And then my second. It was also during these nights that I found out what could save me.

19

Right Behind Me, on the Left

TO THE FIRST FORCE—the first source of positive energy I had created for myself out of silly words, endlessly repeated snippets of poetry, and laughing at death—a second force was added. A gradual realization.

"Think of what you have," I told myself. "Think of what you could lose."

What did I have? Words, deeds, people, and the face of love.

AT FIRST I'd had a feeling of absolute solitude, the conviction that I was alone in my struggle. The impression of seeing only myself and my past, my fears, the dead of my life. I told myself that I'd managed to silence the voice of the temptation of death thanks to my insults, my stubborn pride, and my word games, which kept me alert. But that would not be enough. I knew death was much stronger than that and had not given up the fight. Death was here in the room, and I couldn't move. Death had all the advantages; I had all the handicaps.

Death has no face. On his deathbed, Proust told his house-keeper, "You know, she came: she's fat, quite fat, quite fat and quite black. She's all in black. She's awful and she frightens me."

These words touch the very heart of me. I recognize child-hood in them, the childhood you find again when you're at death's door, whether you are Proust or anyone else. Proust's image of death is not the same as mine, however. We all have our different ways of seeing it. To me, it's an emptiness. But one you can almost touch. In my moments of calm, I decided it was entrenched behind me, on the left, behind all the apparatus of the cardiac monitor, in a spot I couldn't see, naturally, because I couldn't move. But I was convinced it was there. Because this seemed to me the quietest place in the entire room. On the right, there was the sound of the respirator. Facing me, the comings and goings of the nurses, the noise of their activities. Still in front of me, at the far end, to the left, the door opening onto the hallway and the sounds from the room of Mr. Picolino. I wrote this question on the little slate: "Tell me what's behind me, on the left."

I wrote it slowly, painfully, and perhaps not too legibly. I think Bénédicte was the nurse on duty: tall, strong, reassuring, she knew how to talk to me, touch me, how to impart a feeling of trust, se-curity, and competence. Bénédicte: I loved her muscular arms, her direct, clear gaze, the cheerful quality in her voice. Bénédicte: effi-cient almost to the point of brusqueness, but skillful. When she began her shift, I felt renewed hope. When she left me, my anxiety returned.

She deciphered my message, read it aloud, shook her head in puzzlement, and answered quickly, as always, as with everything she did—quickly, precisely, and to the point.

"I don't understand your question. There's nothing behind you, on the left. Nothing!"

That confirmed my intuition. If Bénédicte, the ideal nurse, who never makes mistakes, tells me there is nothing, that means death is there—because death is nothing. And I am the prisoner of this nothing. It has moved into the room with me and I cannot move out.

20

A Road in Algiers and
Four Verses by Saint Bernard

WHENEVER HE'D ENCOUNTERED DEATH, he'd always been on the move, resourceful, cunning, able to parry, counterattack.

IN THE HILLS of Algiers, on a road running straight from Norwood to Naturita in Colorado, on the beaches of Lebanon, behind the sandbags of Cam Ranh Bay, on a sidewalk in the Bronx: each time he had been in command of his body, able to move around, to shift about. You can cheat death. As long as you aren't shut up in the same room with it.

IN ALGIERS, he'd eluded death several times. The closest call had been on the last turn heading up to the Boulevard Bru, at the wheel of a blue-black Peugeot 404. He'd seen a representation of death: two guys in drill trousers, camouflage jackets, and dark glasses. One was on his knees setting up a Bren gun. It was one-fifty in the afternoon.

Luckily, he'd been just that little bit early. As a general rule, they had been strictly advised not to drive through the lower part of the city after two o'clock.

"You want to go swimming and get a tan during your lunch hour? You're nuts," the security guards in the building had said to them, "but it's up to you. Just don't come back later than two o'clock, because after that . . . The gunmen do the same thing, they're as fucked up as you are: they go swimming at lunchtime, but they're back on the job by two. They set up their roadblocks again, no earlier, but never later than that."

There were three or four of them in the building who enjoyed this sport. So, off they'd go. (In two cars: never take only one vehicle.) They'd dive into the pure salt water of all those deserted beaches, with the ghosts of swimmers, the memory of their joy, the phantom music of their vanished accents. Those swimmers had all hopped freighters and planes, and the beaches now belonged to the past. The intruders knew they didn't have much time, and although there was no one there with them, they felt observed and spied upon. So they would dash into the water and then dash back across the terraces of empty bistros with their abandoned chairs and closed metal shutters, through what seemed like an empty world where all the clocks had stopped. Without even bothering to dry themselves, they would bite into the tomatoes they had brought along, and the sardine sandwiches wrapped in paper. They ate standing up, leaning against the open car doors. (You must always keep the doors open to save time when you leave.) They would split a can of beer and take off at top speed, gears screaming and tires squealing. The 404s could take a beating, and they thought themselves invincible.

They had to get back on time. They knew perfectly well they couldn't risk running into a roadblock. They would have had to give their names, which were on the lists drawn up by the Delta, because they worked in the Bru Building, where the radio station was, and everyone who worked in the Bru had been condemned to death by the Delta. Knowing that, when he was tearing through the empty streets, with the taste of tomatoes, sardines, and beer in his mouth, with the hot wind from the sea pouring through the wide-open windows and the midday sun beating down, while he shifted madly through the gears, leaving rubber on the turns, on the asphalt melting in the heat—knowing and feeling all that, with his pal sitting on his right calling out the roads, the intersections, the bumps in the pavement, the streetcar tracks, as if they were in a rally, the most exciting race in the world, well, that was exhilarating, it really revved up his heart. He could also feel, wedged between his right thigh and the torn leather seat, the butt of the small Beretta pistol the security guards in his building had given him in case he got into "deep shit." They hadn't made a similar exception for any of his colleagues, and he was proud to be the only one packing a gun at his belt. That was thrilling, too.

They had reached the last turn before the uphill stretch that passed the Hôtel Saint-Georges on the way to the Bru Building, and he had seen the two men setting up their machine gun. "What do we do?" he'd shouted to his pal, who'd seen them a split-second later: the figures in civvy pants and camo jackets, crouching by their weapon, and the wire entanglement they were going to draw across the road.

"You've no choice!" his friend had shouted back. "Speed up and go through—don't slow down, go straight through, then hang a hard left. Step on the clutch! Downshift and get the hell out! Hurry, hurry, let's go!"

He'd thought he'd heard his friend utter a shrill sound like a war cry or a yelp of fear. He'd felt his entire being respond to the urgency of their situation: feet on the pedals, hands on the wheel and the gearshift, stomach tense, eyes taking it all in— the two gunmen jumping up as he drew closer, the approach of the turn, a glance in the rearview mirror, another at the dashboard. He'd felt in control of all his reflexes. He'd headed straight for the two killers, then whipped into a sharp turn. The men had been forced to leap aside, while the tripod mounting of the Bren gun had gone flying to the side of the road in a cloud of dust and gravel. One of the two men had reached inside his jacket as if to pull out a gun, but it was too late. The image of the killers dwindled rapidly to nothing in the rearview mirror.

They had sped over the invisible boundary line. They had made it across. The nervous excitement he had felt throughout his entire body had lasted long after they had reached the Bru Building. It had taken him the rest of the day to calm down. The heady experience had left an unfamiliar taste on his lips. He told himself that he had gambled with death and won. Anyway, he had never considered the possibility that he might die. Although those gunmen had represented death, he'd thought that his own death was unthinkable. He'd found the whole escapade almost a snap. Naturally: at the time, he had been driving a car, not lying in a hospital bed, the prisoner of nothing. The game had been different, then.

HERE, IN ROOM 29 of the ICU, it isn't a game anymore, but a battle. I must fight, but I can't do it with my hands, or the wheel of a 404, or the brashness of a twenty-three-year-old. I must seek help from other forces that aren't physical, fueled by adrenaline, nerve, pure action.

I found two of them.

One came to me through laughter. Only now and then, of course, but it helped. I laughed to myself several times to fight off resignation. I made fun of myself: my obsessive repetitions, my inability to think things through, the jumble of images assailing me, the inconsequence of my superficial life, so open to criticism.

"You're a total loss, you poor idiot!" I told myself. "Here you are, facing the ultimate test, and all you can come up with are confused images, some mumbled words, and bits of a few poems. You haven't a single coherent thought. You should be doing your best to prepare yourself for the confrontation and encounter with—what? And whom? And all you can do is clown around in your head. You're going gaga! What was the point of all your reading? Your travels, your work, your experiences, romances, failures, and successes? You make me laugh. You're a joke."

This self-mockery helped me as much as the ability to sneer at death with insults and crude language. The second principle of the ICU crossing: we have laughter within us that can help us diminish everything, cut everything down to size. We should consider the four verses of Saint Bernard:

> *Spernere Mundeum*: To laugh at the world
> *Spernere Ipsum*: To laugh at oneself
> *Spernere Neminem*: To laugh at no one
> *Spernere Se Sperni*: To laugh at oneself laughing

These verses of Saint Bernard had been quoted to me nine years earlier, in the pink and misty late-afternoon light of a landscape in the heart of the Landes, by a friend whom I didn't see often enough, but whom I loved for his search for spirituality, and the gift of charity in all his secret good deeds. The words of Saint Bernard came back to me—without difficulty, this time—and took on their full meaning.

But you will need more than the strength of laughter, I thought. Weakened, immobilized, you will need another force to help you chase that *nothing* from your hospital room and drive it from both body and mind. Because you have understood this fundamental rule: if your spirit gives up, your body will, too. For they are inseparable.

Concerning a Harley Davidson and the "Other Side"

THIS IS THE THIRD essential principle revealed to me by my crossing to the other side. When we talk about our bodies in the West, we often say, "the body you have."

In the East, when people talk about their bodies, they say, "the body you are."

This is closer to the truth. I am my body. There is no difference or division between what I think and what I feel, between my mind and the beating of my pulse. Nevertheless, it's my mind, my will that can regulate my pulse. If my will falters, I think my heart and body will falter as well. Suddenly, a new vision: a straight, dusty road beneath a clear sky.

"YOU'LL STOP when you want. It'll be your decision, not mine."

It was more of a long path than a road. A long line, one single track, parallel to the real asphalt road running from Norwood to

Naturita: Route 145 in southwest Colorado. A path of gravel and cinders lying on the hard, yellowish dirt.

The game was dangerous and absurd. You climbed on the back of the Harley driven by Bill. You were handed a red-and-white bandanna, the handkerchief carried by everyone out in the American West, a folded bandanna you were to place over Bill's eyes while he was driving, once he'd set off on a direct course. It was a complicated and perverse game, a crazy game. You would sit behind Bill and guide him while he was blindfolded. He would start up the Harley, go through the gears, and head down that long straight line. Once he'd really gotten going, you would tie the bandanna over his eyes, and it was up to you to watch the track and decide when you should tear off the blindfold, to keep the motorcycle—and you—from speeding off the path or missing the turn at the end. To keep the bike from crashing into death.

"It's your decision. You're in charge, not me. I just go straight ahead. If you feel we're going off track or getting too close to the curve, you tear off the bandanna. Me, I'm ready to drive blind as far as possible, if you can guide me. You'll be my eyes."

He had wondered why he'd agreed to play this stupid, twisted game. What was the point of it?

"You see how long you can go before you get scared and have to take off my blindfold. That way you're timing your trip into fear."

Bill was relaxed, happy to explain the how and why of this deadly game perfected by the Oakland chapter of the Hell's Angels, a game they had played back in California on a level beach of sand as hard as cement, over by Carmel. It was a rite of passage. If the new guy lasted more than a few seconds before losing his nerve, he was admitted to the chapter, accepted as a brother.

"Anyway, we can't go on for too long, because even though I know my bike inside out and know I can go straight ahead for more than thirty seconds, I lose it, too, at some point, but I can't holler to you to take off the blindfold because if I yell first, I'm a disgrace to the chapter. You got that or not? Plus, all this proves we're a team. You know, it's like a solidarity thing."

"Of course," he thought, "naturally, all this bullshit, sure, fine, but what's it got to do with me and why did I ever get involved in this mess?"

It was six in the afternoon, a good time, according to Bill, because you had the sun at your back, on the other side of the track behind Norwood, and because at that hour (still according to Bill) you didn't need to worry about the single state police patrol car turning up. At that time of day, you could count on the two cops being fifty miles to the south, relaxing with a beer in the only saloon in Ouray. The bikers knew the cops' schedule down to the last minute. So the coast was clear, but that still didn't explain why he had agreed to participate in this lunatic game. Maybe it was because he had shown too much interest in their description of it, that evening when he had sat at the tough guys' table in the mess tent at the campground and been "recruited" without realizing what was going on. And now these guys—Steve, Dick, Bill, Hatchet Face—were making him repeat his instructions, after they'd sat him down on the back of the Harley.

"Right, let's go through it one last time, okay?"

His anxious doubts were swept away by a feeling of exhilaration. Suddenly, he thought it was great, the most dangerous stunt he'd ever tried to pull, and he felt that he wasn't doing it to impress the bikers or so that he could boast about it later on, when he went back to France, telling his older brothers all about it in the cozy family apartment in Paris. They wouldn't even believe him, the whole thing was so crazy. No, if he was doing it, it was for himself alone, to find out what difference there really was between his body and his fear, his body and his willpower. To find out whether or not he could make this kind of decision. At least this was a real test, much more dangerous than all the others he had encountered since arriving in camp at the end of June. He had been there only two months, yet it seemed like a lifetime. Hatchet Face—who looked like a knife-thrower or a hitman with his black sideburns, those two vertical creases running down his cheeks, and long, sharp canines that gave him the snaggle-toothed grin of a hunting dog—made sure he had understood what to do.

"It's a contest between your willpower and your fear. Got that?"

The weather was fine and dry, not quite as hot as it had been at the beginning of the summer. As they stood there in their black Acme boots with steel buckles, the wind from the mountains whipped their pants legs and flicked at the collars of their Schott jackets, collars turned up in the style of bikers and riffraff from the northwest coast of California. The men smelled of tobacco, frying grease, and cheap aftershave, but sometimes these odors yielded to the stronger scent of the surrounding birches and pines, and the smell of the wild grasses. No one else knew about this track, which lay in the heart of a narrow valley, between two squat little mountains.

His heart was pounding when he took his seat behind Bill on the Harley: he thought it was excitement before the ride, not fear. Bill started up the bike, moved onto the track, and picked up speed. Leaning around Bill's left side, he could see the speedometer climb rapidly to eighty miles an hour. He felt Bill's back stiffen and heard him yell, "Whenever you're ready!"

He started to place the bandanna over the other man's eyes exactly as Hatchet Face had told him to, but found he couldn't do it.

"I can't, Bill, I can't, we'll crash! I can't do it!"

"It's up to you," Bill yelled back. It was over. The Harley slowed down and turned around on the track. Steve, Dick, and Hatchet Face came to meet them.

"What happened?" asked Hatchet Face.

Bill spoke before his passenger could answer.

"It was his move. He decided not to do it."

The bikers looked at him in silence. He had been afraid they would smile, call him chicken, ostracize him. But it wasn't like that. They stood there quietly, impassively, waiting to hear his explanation. At the moment of blindfolding Bill, he had felt a violent and irresistible sensation of refusal. He wanted to say that, say it as simply as possible, because out West, you don't waste words, and you don't lie much, either.

"I was afraid, but it was more than that. I wanted to stop. You told me it was my willpower up against my fear. Well, it was deliberate, that's all: I decided it wasn't worth it."

He thought he saw new understanding in their faces. Only Hatchet Face spoke up, without irony, but with a kind of pointed emphasis.

"Okay, you decided, but you were scared. You were afraid to see what it was like on the other side."

He looked at Hatchet Face, who must have been four or five years older than he was but who already seemed like an old man who'd seen it all: he'd been in enough fights and weathered enough blows and wounds to be light years away from the callow French kid who replied, "That must be it."

When the campground closed, the four bikers had decided to stay together as they drifted across the West, wandering from job to job, from one stop-gap to another, and they hadn't asked him to come along. It was clear to them that he would be going back to his college campus.

"You're going home, what else," they said to him matter-of-factly.

He looked at them. Don't forget these faces, he told himself, you'll never see a single one of them again. When they said goodbye, he understood that the men had already distanced themselves from him long before. He wasn't their kind. He had a life ahead of him, plans and ambitions. All that lay ahead of them was the road, and night, dust, violence—a realistic vision of what little life could still offer them. He had not regretted his decision. He was happy to have felt afraid on Bill's motorcycle. He was proud of having accepted his fear. In that way, he had mastered his body. Fear had allowed him to pull back from the absurdity into which these men—these hatchet-faced men with their long, sharp faces—had tried to plunge him.

I SEE HATCHET FACE AGAIN, lost in my past, anonymous, wild—and suddenly he seems more present than the dozens of faces that have returned to parade before me in the constant ebb and flow of memory, in the chaos that has periodically overwhelmed me since I entered the ICU. Why him? Because he'd used an expression that has now taken on a dimension beyond that of a mere motorcycle stunt, an idiotic Hell's Angels ritual. Hatchet Face had said, "the other side."

I'd taken this for a cliché, at the time, a superstitious way of talking about getting close to death. The words now surge back into my mind, in Hatchet Face's voice—"the other side"—and I realize that ever since I woke up in the ICU, everything that has been welling up from my memory and my past has a meaning. I had thought it was all a muddle, but there is nothing haphazard about the images appearing before me.

IT'S BECAUSE a crude biker roaming the American West once spoke of "the other side" that his nameless and crapulent face has won out over all the others, from the most famous to the utterly unknown.

Hatchet Face winds up at the top of my fragmentary memory's hit parade. He's ahead of my father's patrician mien, and the despairing violet eyes of Alice, who personified the vitality of New York before finishing alone in a hotel room at Madison and Sixty-fifth Street. He's ahead of that giant of film who became my teacher and died in my arms in a Paris restaurant. He's ahead of Valdo with his gaunt cheeks, Valdo who was my model when I was twenty and just starting out in Paris, Valdo who tried all his life to recapture the popularity that had once made him the little prodigy of the press—but who tried in vain, and in the end, hanged himself. He's ahead of the singer with whom I once spent three months in absolute complicity: cigarettes, peppermint schnapps, pop songs composed in a single burst of inspiration at his black piano, white nights that plumbed the depths of the ridiculous and—sometimes—the depraved. He's ahead of the chinstrap beard on the long jaws of Boby, Françoise's father, my children's grandfather, whose humor and affection, humility and sense of the transience of life have profoundly affected our family. He's ahead of a great writer I once met, an old man whose swollen and exhausted face grew animated as he spoke, transfigured by words of such power that in leaving him I thought, I'm now less of a fool than I was a few hours ago. He's ahead of the bristling white crewcut and square, rugged face of Jacoto, the Dark

Man, a mythic figure of my childhood who came to talk to my father at night in the villa about things I didn't understand. He's ahead of the faded film star who called me to his hotel room the night before he was to play a love scene in a film I was directing, and explained to me with tears in his eyes, standing in front of the mirror, that he was too old to play the seducer anymore and that no one would believe in it.

"Look, just look at my face! I can't pull it off anymore. Look at the bags under my eyes, my flabby cheeks, look at those wrinkles—how can you expect to make people believe she'll fall in love with me?"

And I had the sudden premonition that perhaps we wouldn't be able to, after all, and that the film—no matter how much talent and effort he'd put into it, and we'd all put into it—would be a flop. But I also felt that it wasn't just the actor who was the problem. The problem was me, and the mistake was in the film scenario itself. In my pretension, my sin of pride.

All these faces streamed past, faster and faster, from the angelic little girl suffocated by a mudslide and laid out by her mother in a piece of white cloth, to the young draftees mown down by machine-gun fire from the backs of armored trucks in the streets of Bab el-Oued, who seemed astonished, when we found them, with their eyes wide in amazement at the discovery of death . . .

None of these faces knew what it would look like, that "other side" Hatchet Face had mentioned and to which they had all crossed over. If a force or wish outside of my control has decided to bring Hatchet Face and his three little words back to me in my present state, to make these words and this image count for as much as everything I have been able to see and understand since then, it must be because he said it better than anyone—this cliché, this "other side." His voice out of nowhere spoke more truly than everything that followed . . .

I HAVE ALREADY crossed once to the other side, in the black tunnel. Was it tonight? Last night? I can't remember anymore. As for the different times I've been afraid, in Colorado or Algeria, or during the police investigations in Dallas, they don't come anywhere near the fear I felt, and stifled, in this bed, in this room with yellow walls, in this struggle, this loss of every connection with the passage of time, with people, appointments, my work, my children, and peaceful, everyday life. It's because the young man I was and the man I am now have so little in common. The young man didn't know what he might lose when he defied death. Even if a certain rational foresight did prevent him from going any further in that absurd motorcycle game, he did not have enough to lose to be afraid of losing. Whereas bedridden, ill, the man I am now can feel the weight of what he might lose, the weight of life. And that explains my anguish. It weighs on my heart.

So, here we go—now it's my heart?

I have pushed the call button. It seemed to me that not only were the respirator and I no longer breathing together but that my heart was weakening as well, for I felt a sharp twinge between my ribs, near the thorax. Alerted by the nurse and the machine, the intern tries to reestablish a better breathing pattern. The conversation, as usual, is between those who can speak and my little slate.

"Not doing well tonight," I write. "My heart's giving out."

"Your heart isn't the problem," replies the intern calmly. "It's working fine. It's your breathing that's important. You're here for a respiratory illness, not cardiac trouble. Try to work with the machine."

"Yes," I write, "but, anxiety."

"There's no reason for you to be anxious," he says, and turns toward the wall to show me a short, handwritten letter taped there by the nurse.

"Can you read this from the bed?"

I shake my head.

"Your wife brought it to you. Do you remember your wife's last visit?"

I nod.

"Do you want me to read it to you again?"

I nod, and he reads it aloud.

"Happy Father's Day, Papa, from your loving children."

Then, like an antidote to anguish, the words, the gestures, and the face of love return to me. First defense: will and resistance. Second defense: laughter. Third defense: love.

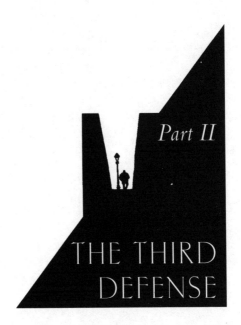

Part II

THE THIRD
DEFENSE

22

It's Very Hard to Put Yourself in Other People's Places

THE OTHER PEOPLE are the ones I love and who love me.

First of all, there is my wife. She comes to see me regularly. I'm not sure I can accurately count her visits: one, two, three times a day? I can't keep track of whole days—how can I count up visits? I begin to think of them as flashes of light in the darkness. The excess of emotion that had so upset me and provoked her departure that first time is now matched by the longing with which I hope and pray for her visits.

I frequently think I hear her talking out in the hallway. I think I hear the sound of her footsteps, which only I would recognize, and yet, quite often, she doesn't come through the door. But if I have believed her to be there, it's because I needed to believe this, and even the idea of this need has helped me. I can't manage to see what clothes she's wearing, especially since she must put on the obligatory green or blue hospital gown. But I'm certain that she is neatly dressed in a style that suits her perfectly, one that is neither in nor out of fashion. Likewise, even though I can see only part of her face, since she is wearing the same mask as the nurses and interns, I imagine her hairdo and makeup: nothing ostentatious, but a reflection of that care, that flair for the best way of doing things that is a part of her personality. And no matter when she visits me, in the morning before leaving for work, or in the evening, when she is on her way home, I am sure that she is—I'm looking for the *mot juste*—impeccable. I am sure of it because I know that she was brought up like that, brought up to have self-respect, to reject the second-rate, to believe that one should not put one's pain, care, and sorrow on display but instead show the world a face and appearance of composure and self-command.

It isn't a question of simply putting up a front. It's an approach to life, rather, to its joys and tragedies, its triumphs and disappointments. Not only has she been raised like this, she has molded herself in this way. She has her own system of values, her own standards and rules, beliefs, spiritual needs, artistic tastes. She brings this ethic with her when she comes to see me: she is focused, convinced that life will win out, entirely committed to imparting this faith to me. She comes armed with her experience as a woman, with her love, with the fortitude she has exhibited from the moment I fell ill and tumbled into the unknown. She comes to see me in the ICU determined to transmit her life force to me. A smile in her eyes, confidence in her voice, and serenity, of course—a calm voice, gentle and firm, full of intonations intended to make me understand that I must not give up, that I am not alone. She knows that the man she loves is a mass of contradictory worries, of exasperating sensitivity. I'm the one who "needs to know," who has always wanted to be "in the thick of things," to be *au courant*, to have his finger on the pulse of the times. The one who is always asking, "What's new?" and saying, "Tell me about it!" I'm the one who cannot live without a telephone, without communication. She knows I can't bear my profound ignorance about my own condition, and she knows that ignorance must magnify my anxieties. I can sense this in her voice, her words. And just as I felt shaken by waves of great danger, I feel waves of lucidity when she is at my side.

"If she is reaching out to you like that," I tell myself, "you must somehow respond to her gesture, no matter what you look like at this moment, with your tubes and your machine."

So, either through the plastic slate and felt-tip pen, or by squeezing her hand, or moving my head, I try to show that I am with her, that she is getting through to me, that I understand.

She is the only one I understand really well. First she explained to me how I was doing, repeating what the doctors had told her, that they had identified the illness and were thus now able to target it more precisely and efficiently with the proper medication, but that it would be a while yet before the tubes were removed. I had been told all that during the day, but it had not sunk in. Now that she is relaying it to me, I can grasp the information, and I believe her. There is a goal: five days, five nights? A week of days and nights? Now, at least, I have some certainties, a project. I take things in slowly, one by one. Then she brings me news of the children, friends, the circles of affection, support, or sympathy that surround her. How "the others" are doing.

"If you think you're suffering and that more suffering lies ahead," I reflect, "just ask yourself how terrible it must be for her and the children. Try to put yourself in her place, in their place."

Easy to say! An expression you hear often, so it has lost its full meaning from being trotted out anytime and anywhere by anyone at all. A fine, impossible proposition: "Try to put yourself in my place."

How many of us truly and sincerely attempt to understand what that would be like? I haven't the strength, but I do realize this: the visit of this person I love and who loves me has allowed me, for the first time since the beginning of my ICU crossing, to think of another living soul besides myself. Since she has been here, I have stopped obsessing about myself, pitying myself, worrying about myself, wallowing in my indifference to everything but myself. Until now, the only people whose words and images have occupied my thoughts have been dead people. Now I'm thinking about the living, about those closest to me in this life. About those I might lose.

The Fourth Principle

EVEN THOUGH IT'S DIFFICULT, if not impossible, to *put yourself in someone else's place* when you are grappling with the stupefying experience of a serious illness, weaving in and out of consciousness, trying not to lose heart as you are swept along that dark river, still, you must make the attempt.

I can manage only with difficulty and only for a short while. But I force myself, and each time I succeed, it becomes meaningful. This will gradually create a kind of refuge, a haven from the waves of fever and despair, from the chaotic flood of memory, a victory over death. I think only about small things, small gestures that mostly concern my family. My wife and children. The ritual of morning breakfast. The cups and bowls set out all around the gleaming wooden table, the napkins in their rings, the apartment awakening . . . Life begins there, in that modest kitchen, with the arrival of first one, then the other drowsy, slightly pouty child, with that inexhaustible and always vital savor of the first little caresses, the good-morning kiss, a hand smoothing their hair, the small body—still warm from sleep—that comes to give you a hug.

Sometimes the child (who is no longer a child, already a young girl, yet still "the child") pushes you away, not with hostility but with that peculiar reluctance of a still slumberous body, a desire for independence that is unspoken but clearly felt: "Let me emerge from my night, from my dreams, from my unease at being who I am. Let me collect myself again before I speak to you, even with love, and before I reach out to you, even with affection."

Setting out in the morning, coming home in the afternoon. I imagine them, now, with their friends, boys and girls, in class and after school. I try to put myself in their place. What importance do they give to everything they know, or don't know? What has their mother said to them? What has she told them of their father's condition, when there is some improvement, or no change, or a setback? How are they dealing with something I can't imagine but that does happen—the phones ringing, even very late at night? What about the cryptic phrases, the veiled references? Has she explained it all to them? Did she keep to herself the most worrisome aspect of all this—that it was a mystery the doctors had not yet solved? She must be confiding in one or two of her best friends, and I know where the telephones are, in which rooms, and how the children can hear everything.

BEING ABLE to imagine briefly the familiar setting of home helped me for a moment in my darkness. I wasn't thinking of myself, feeling sorry for myself, giving in to that pervasive complacency brought on by pain and fear. Realizing this, I try harder to evoke "the others," those I love and who love me, whose names knock on the window of my apparent incomprehension whenever my wife mentions them during each of her visits.

"J. and S. invited the children over for dinner last night to give me a rest. P. and G. send you a kiss and call every day. Alexandra is fantastic, she canceled a trip to stay with me. She sends you a kiss, and so does Valérie. All your brothers have called."

To this litany of names of those close to me are added other names from a wider circle of colleagues and acquaintances, those with whom I work or whom I meet in the overlapping worlds of my life and who send me a sign in the only way they can, through my wife. Has she understood or decided that it might help me, hearing these names that make up the fabric of a life and that had completely slipped my mind for several days and nights? I'd no longer been aware, in fact, that I was surrounded by several circles of friends, associates, even distant friends I hadn't seen or heard from in a long time who have suddenly turned up again after learning what has happened. I had forgotten them, because they are alive and I'd been concerned only with the dead, to whom I felt so close. I'd been obsessed by the dead of my life: they were the ones in my room, not the others.

But now they are gone. My smiling and affable visitors seem never to have returned from the cafeteria where I had thought they'd gone for a snack before returning to urge me once more to join them on the other side. They have been replaced by the living, by all these names my wife reels off, giving me a kind of connection to what is being said and done on the side of life, which makes me think about them, makes me want to hang on to them and see them again. Names mean faces, smiles, moments of complicity and understanding. I feel the tug of all that binds me to life: my work, my plans, my hopes for the future.

"J. met with S. and O. and they arranged for things to go smoothly while you're gone. J. told me particularly to let you know and tell you not to worry about anything. It's all taken care of and everything will be fine."

I hadn't been worried about that. In the beginning, everything that made up my professional life had vanished, while the only thing to resurface had been all the rest: my past. And the fear of death. But now, it's as though a tiny drop of daily life is being given to me along with the intravenous drip.

FOURTH PRINCIPLE: When you are with a patient tormented by anxiety over his own life, and by the loneliness this anxiety entails, don't tell him only that you love him. Tell him as well that others love him, too, and talk about them to him. Speak to him of one of the beauties of life: speak to him of the living. Because if he crosses that mysterious threshold beyond which he becomes a stranger to you and to others, then the world of the living will seem to him like sheer absurdity. Keep him from falling into that absurdity and encourage him gently to think about everything he owes to those who love him and whom he loves. Make him understand that your love, like that of others, or his love for them, is worth fighting to live for.

24

Florence's Wish

YOU ALSO RECEIVE this saving love from those to whom you are a stranger. From the women who take care of you. Nurse's aides, nursing assistants, or nurses—CCRNs, to be specific, and to give them their full title, Critical Care Registered Nurses.

There are those who lavish only strictly practical attentions on you: bathing, toileting. They help the others, the ones in charge of seeing that everything in your medical care runs smoothly and who have the major responsibility, performing the most delicate and important tasks. But I don't make any distinctions according to hierarchy, ranking, seniority, or power. To me they are all the same: they are all my superiors. I know nothing, they know everything. They are superior to all the other women who are bustling around outside at that very moment, in the street, in offices, stores, studios, in that city I have forgotten all about.

Is there a city? Is there a sky? Does it have a color? Are there sounds—and what are they? I have forgotten everything about daily life in the city: the hum of traffic on the boulevards, the stop-and-go rhythm at intersections, the flood of gleaming metal and the flux of men and women across cement and asphalt, apartment floors, the rubberized walkways in airports, carpeted hotel rooms, kitchen tiles, and the flagstones of churches. I no longer think of nature, either. Are there trees? Birds and rivers? The outside world is less than nothing to me. It's dead. Where I live, there is no outside world. There is something else, there is that other side where I've been tossed, conscripted, imprisoned by some unknown power. There is only a white or yellow room with shifting dimensions that seem to reflect my fears and suffering, and moving within this room, there are women whose arrivals and departures punctuate what little sense I manage to make of time or the passing hours. Young women with ordinary names, ordinary faces, but theirs have become the most important faces of that fragile, transitory thing—the unfolding, second by second, of life.

Sometimes they seem enormous to me, towering, gigantic, with strong hands capable of moving me, turning me over, manipulating me the way a baker's boy kneads dough that will turn into bread. I hear them sometimes, giving instructions like guides or conductors.

"Breathe more slowly. Get back into your rhythm. Don't let yourself become so excited."

One of them is doing her best to swab my lips and the back of my throat, to combat the many sores that have invaded my mouth, adding to the other secondary effects of my illness. Something in me is resisting. At first I don't understand what she wants. Then I'm afraid of opening my mouth too wide, because I could lose this tube that is absolutely necessary to me. My body tenses up under any circumstance and on any pretext. I grit my teeth and fight against the painstaking task the young woman is attempting to carry out. She tries several times, with gentle firmness and the doggedness of a craftsman who won't be satisfied until the job is done, no matter what. The young woman could give up, grow impatient, treat me more roughly, even hurt me. Instead of which, I hear her speak to me with uncommon politeness and precision.

"I wish to reach your palate."

I haven't seen her before. One of her colleagues may perhaps have called her Florence a little while ago. I don't really notice the delicacy and concision of her words at that moment, but later on, I will remember them as one of the most beautiful examples of how deeply these women understand life. An appropriate phrase—spoken in a tone of authority, persuasive yet sympathetic—that will momentarily relax me. I cooperate better. I stop clenching my teeth and half open my mouth, not for long, but long enough for Florence to get her "wish": she can "reach my palate."

And then I love her, because her serene and subtle words have helped me as much as the medicine itself. In this brief respite when the machine and I are working well together, without the coughing fits that clog the tubes and bring on a bodily distress that sets off the alarm—in this moment when one could say that, in the grip of this disease, I'm "doing quite well"—I feel boundless love for these women. I want to let them know this, to express my gratitude for their stamina, their expertise, their efficiency, the care with which they follow orders, and all this in spite of the weariness, resignation, or even exasperation with which they face the monotony of their lives.

How can I tell them that I understand what it's like for them to do their jobs every day: arriving early in the morning or late at night to relieve the previous shift, commuting in from the suburbs already burdened with the worries or problems of their own lives. Children, husband. No children, no husband. Money, no money. Too much solitude, or not enough. Love, or none. Parents: difficult, or absent, or only too present. Lack of material comfort, administrative difficulties, a great deal of effort, and little satisfaction. Lots of gray shadows. Not much sunshine. The organization chart waiting for them with the plan of care to be followed for each patient: a long, complicated, detailed plan, even if they know it by heart, even if they have been here for a long time. It's always complicated, because they mustn't make a single mistake, mustn't be careless or inattentive for a moment. And then there is this patient, flat on his back, in the way and in a bad way, unable to speak, half human, half thing, and who grabs you by the wrist, entreats you with his eyes, as though you could fix everything. This patient who depends entirely on you, whom you must treat like a baby, like a wounded soldier, like the other patients, the ones who were there before him and those who will follow him. This stranger.

The stranger is not in any condition to look at it this way: it isn't that they love you, they are just doing their job. In the stranger's eyes, their job isn't "a job." I want to believe that they bring to it a devotion that amounts to a kind of love, and even if I'm wrong, even if you can argue that they are simply doing what they are supposed to do, the meaning I give to their actions is the only thing that counts. I welcome them as a sign that I have not been abandoned, that I am not lost. The way one welcomes love, the real kind, the one that proves itself. To tell them so, I wiggle my right hand to ask for the slate, on which I write, "Thank you."

They read this and reply, with just a hint of irritation, "You already thanked us yesterday, at the same time."

They turn to go. The way they have answered me has abruptly changed my mind. A new cycle now begins, as violent and unexpected as the surge of love I had felt for these women. They have barely left the room when some demon begins whispering in my ear.

"They don't love you. They don't want to help you at all. They even want to kill you."

25

Something Has Happened to
Mr. Picolino

I KNOW THIS DEMON. I can identify it. It's the voice of fear, of
paranoia. It's the voice that drags you away from life. It has been a
while since I've heard this voice. I thought I had stifled it, shut its
ugly mouth. It's back, as cloying and insinuating as ever. It says a
terrible thing to me.

"These girls don't give a fuck about you. They want your death."

The return of this voice has me in despair. I'm not tough enough
to fight it off. I believe what it tells me. With the same sudden and
jarring implosion of time, I find myself right back in my prison of
fear.

I am even more afraid because I can hear a different silence
around the room. Doors open, close. There is something going on
out in the hallway of the ICU. Then, silence again. The girls come
and go at a different rhythm. They speak quietly, intently, as though
they were consulting one another. I find that suspicious. What's happening? Is it a plot? Until now, they've never bothered to lower their

voices when talking among themselves, as though I couldn't possibly understand them. And now they're whispering. What are they trying to hide from me? I can pick up just a few words.

"Dialysis . . . It's over . . . We'll have to tell . . . But there isn't anyone . . . No one came to see him . . ."

I hear a name that abruptly reminds me that the world doesn't revolve exclusively around my august person.

"Mr. Picolino . . ."

The nurses are talking about my neighbor, the man I've never seen and now will never see, because I realize in a flash of insight that something fatal has happened to him. There is a muffled agitation in the next room and out in the corridor. I can sense it more than see it, since I can see practically nothing, but I feel as though I am able to grasp what is happening without needing to see it. How clear it has all suddenly become! I understand everything: the nurse wasn't brusque with me when I wrote, "Thank you," she was merely more preoccupied with her other patient than she was with me. She didn't want to kill me, but when the idea of death surfaced like that to disturb my impulsive feelings of love, it was because at the very moment when the voice of negation was saying that word ("They want your death"), it was happening a few feet away from me, on the other side of the wall between our two rooms. I'm convinced that's what happened: at the precise instant when Mr. Picolino breathed his last—something that had been expected for a long time, but which I had been too overwhelmed by my own voyage to envision—that death had crossed from Mr. Picolino's room into my own to remind me, through an inner voice, that death exists.

It's nearby. It prowls in the silent corridor. Yes, I'm sure of it now, this is the dead of night, the late hour when the ICU hallway gives off one of those dry, unfathomable silences in which you no longer have the slightest feeling of belonging to humanity. An unnatural silence, since there is never true silence in nature. And even though the door to my room is closed, I manage to hear and understand the whiteness and the blackness of this silence. This doesn't astonish me. Nothing astonishes me. I am beyond astonishment.

No one came to see Mr. Picolino. I say to myself, you really noticed that part: he was all alone, and you will never know what he looked like. His name sounded silly and pathetic, and when his machine set off a different alarm than yours, you were able for a few fleeting seconds to imagine him as a little guy, "piccolo," a swarthy old man who smiled, perhaps, in the midst of his unhappiness. Why did you imagine him smiling? Mr. Picolino hadn't any reason to smile, since no one came to see him. But people come to see you. The nurses have never used the words *no one* about you. There is a whole current of love flowing around you. You've realized that. In the murky depths of the ocean you're crossing, you've finally satisfied yourself of this indisputable fact: you are not alone. You will not be upset by Mr. Picolino's departure. It may even, in a cruel way, do you some good. Because now you will keep saying to yourself, me, I'm not like Mr. Picolino. I have people. I haven't got "no one." I'll be okay.

26

A Strange Verb Makes
Its Appearance

IT'S MORNING, I think. There is light in the room. Several men in white are leaning over me, along with several men in green. They keep saying "Good morning" to me, and I realize that they are doing this so that I will return their greeting, at least by nodding my head. To show them clearly that I can understand what they have come to tell me. I do what they want and nod, "Good morning."

I recognize several of these men. One is the intern who came often during my nights of anguish, the one who assured me that my heart was in good shape and endlessly repeated that hateful advice, "Work with the machine."

Another man, wearing glasses, was already hovering over my face when I emerged from the anesthesia after the bronchoscopy, the first time I woke up in the ICU. He is the one who presided over my entry—or rather, my reentry—into the atmosphere. He speaks slowly, calmly, articulating the words as if he were speaking to a child.

"The medications we have been giving you since we identified the bacterium seem to have begun having an effect. And it looks as though the swelling in your larynx is going down. Your breathing appears to be improving. We are going to try extubating you in two days."

Extubate: a strange verb I'll be hearing often in the hours to come. Sometimes the word will be deformed. Certain nurses will pronounce it "extubulate." The news simply means that they are going to try taking out the silicone tube that links me to the respirator. *Extubation* will become the key word in the next few hours and days that I have no way of counting, since my notion of time is no longer like everyone else's. The news should encourage me. Oddly enough, I receive it with skepticism: nothing of all this is certain, nothing is definite. It's as if I were refusing the solution the doctors have envisaged for me.

It's not that I don't have confidence in the man speaking to me. But I sense his caution, his desire to speak only the truth, and to make me understand that this truth is fragmentary, in a process of evolution. I particularly noticed that he said, "We are going to try . . ." And I hear other things.

"The nature of your microbe . . . Enough to reduce the inflammation . . . We cannot ventilate you much longer . . . Risk of lesions . . ."

I leave them. The men in white and green are busy talking among themselves now, not to me. Their faces fade, melt away, while I go elsewhere, deeper into myself than I have ever gone before, into that semicomatose state that has surely spared me much suffering but has regularly brought me into the realm of nightmare, and of all that I never wish to see again.

Yet it's at this moment, and in this condition, after learning of my coming extubation, that I will experience a new stage in my crossing to the other side. The most incredible part of my journey.

Indescribable, perhaps.

But I'm going to try to describe it.

A Tunnel of Light

I FEEL MYSELF leaving my body. I seem to see myself on the bed, surrounded by men in white coats and green scrubs; standing behind them are the nurses and nurse's aides. I see the entire room, the objects, the walls, the machine, and the monitors. I can describe these people with laserlike precision: hair, shape of the nose, shirt cuffs beneath the surgical gowns, blond curls, latex gloves, masks, blue-dotted material of the masks . . .

And then, I see myself lying on the bed: I'm quite thin, terribly jaundiced, and my face is cluttered with tubes and gauze pads that seem to divide it into separate sections. I'm unshaven. My cheeks are very gray. Gray and ashen. The truth is, I'm not a pretty sight. I rise a little higher and float up around the ceiling, hovering over my body, and I hear, more clearly than a moment earlier, everything that is said, the instructions given, the questions asked about the course of treatment, the schedule set for the extubation (forty-eight hours later, in the morning). In cinematic terms, you could say I have a high-angle shot of the whole scene.

I HAVE WORKED as a film director, I have made seven films, I know how to show the audience the same action or characters in a thousand different ways. There are lenses that allow you to isolate a single detail, present a face in close-up, or, conversely, encompass the entire scene. There are also all sorts of shots—zoom, pan, tracking—that provide still other ways of reproducing each character's position and movements, and this can give you the feeling, when you're directing, of creating the world, of controlling it. This may explain the megalomania that comes over those directors who think the world revolves around them, since they make their own little worlds go around. Well, that is just what I'm doing while I float above the doctors, my bed, the nurses, the room, and—most of all—myself. I have become a camera circling around myself. I am a camera: it's rather a facile phrase, but what does it mean? It isn't my eyes that have seen my body on the bed, surrounded by doctors. It's my mind, it's what inhabits my brain—or is it something else, for which none of us can find a name?

This phenomenon doesn't last. Without any transition, I cease being a spectator and find myself enclosed within my body once more. And now this body and this mind, which are but one, are swept into the same tunnel-shaped hole that had so frightened me once before.

There is nothing forbidding about the tunnel anymore. Not only does it not slope downward, but it seems to rise gently, in a welcoming ascent. Besides, it is bright, growing lighter and lighter, and becoming so luminous that I am blinded by its radiance and now see only this: light. As when I tried, as a little child, to look directly at the sun, long enough so that my retinas were bathed only in white, in golden illumination. It would cost me dearly whenever I used to play this idiotic game, a solitary and dangerous stunt that sometimes left me unable to read or even see, unable to focus my eyes for more than an hour. I would be in pain. My eyes would fill with tears. Black lines would striate my vision of people and things. The irritated membranes drove me to rub my eyelids, but the more I rubbed, the more I paid the price for my destructive desire to look light full in the face.

Here, now, there is no pain at all. The light imparts to me a serenity such as I haven't known since I entered the ICU, since I found myself enduring the respirator and the blood draws, the choking fits and the chaos. I feel only a surprising and comforting peace, and an even greater love than what I had already been feeling for my dear ones and others. This love is indescribable. I would like to be able to give it away, to offer it around as though it were honey, but everywhere I turn, there is only radiance. It's as though there were veils of light, passages and streams of whiteness, something diaphanous, something crystalline. There is no one until, fleetingly, vague forms appear.

I think I glimpse, if not faces, at least the suggestion of faces. They don't remind me of anyone important in my life, now or in the past. Actually, they are merely outlines, rough sketches, nothing definite, and if I tried to touch them, I would not succeed, they would draw back from my hand. They have no features, no mouths, noses, eyes, chins. Across these outlines flicker the barest hints of smiles. Like simple drawn lines. These smooth faces seem imbued with the essence of a smile. Not the smile itself, but its spirit, and instead of the sardonically cackling top-men of my voyage into darkness, my entrance into this whiteness introduces me to sweeping horizons, where I soar aloft, uplifted by compassion, tenderness, and understanding.

It's as though I were reliving my first crossing in reverse. During that first voyage, I had plunged dizzily into a black hole that led only to horror and from which I had been desperate to escape. Now, however, no voice is urging me to leave that glowing white space, so loving and fraternal. I might even feel tempted to journey deeper into this nebula of light, to make myself at home there, since it's doing me so much good.

But it doesn't last.

28

It Did Happen

IT LASTS NO LONGER than the phase during which I became a camera. There is no transition. No real time has passed between the instant when I was thrust into that light and enveloped in a vast feeling of love—and the instant of my return: the bed, the tubes, the machine I can hear working noisily, the cruel and isolated world of the ICU. I feel as though I have come back from a quantum leap into something ineffable, back to the same painful, exhausted, anxious, and comatose condition as before.

Recognizing all the familiar discomforts, pains, restraints, and indignities tormenting my body, I might even begin to believe that this voyage into the light never really happened.

But it did happen. It happened to me. I went there and I came back.

The Hollow Man

AS THE TIME for my extubation approaches, I fall prey to conflicting emotions.

First of all, hope. Hope speaks in the same tone as the voice of will, which quieted the voice of sadness and the temptation of death. And hope says simple, repetitive things to me, as repetitive as the word *extubation* that ricochets around in my head like a billiard ball.

"Hang on, only two more days. You're not drifting into unconsciousness as often as you once did. You're recognizing people and things more easily. You can even keep better track of time, of the different nurses' shifts, of your wife's visits. You're working more calmly with the respirator. Hang on: in two days, extubation—and you'll go on to a new stage."

"Which one?"

"It doesn't matter. You'll be less of a prisoner, not so tied down and dependent."

Yet at the same time, I also feel utterly exhausted.

My will may be telling me to hang on, but I'm no longer hanging on to anything—except the call button I keep pressing so that someone will come "suction" me. I can't feel my arms, legs, or feet anymore; can't feel the bruises covering my forearms. I can feel only my chest and larynx, the two sites of my pain. I feel only my back and ribs, which have been so buffeted by my coughing fits. The ribs have hung on. The body has hung on. Although we are unbelievably fragile, we possess a strength that is equally unsuspected. These two contradictory truths tell the whole story of my voyage: Frailty took me to the other side of the mirror. Strength brought me back. I held on, I held on, but I have arrived completely spent at the end of my journey, my crossing, to face this important procedure they are going to perform on me. And all sorts of questions pile in on top of my fatigue.

"What if they can't manage to extubate you? You heard that bitchy Karen the Korean talking about you with her partner tonight, and you heard what they said: 'But it's not at all definite that they'll be able to extubate him, you know—it doesn't always work out!' So, what if Karen is right, and they can't do it? You heard the word *tracheotomy* the other day, when the doctors gathered around you weren't aware that you could hear them. What would happen in that case? Into what other dimension are they going to drag your body now? And can it hold out?"

HE HAD ALWAYS asked himself too many questions.

He had always seen his life as an adventure, a voyage into the unknown to satisfy his immense curiosity about the world. But he had always concealed the fact that this curiosity was the twin sister of a kind of constant uneasiness. As a little boy; an adolescent; a student lost in the middle of an unfamiliar America; a journalist just starting out in his profession, becoming seasoned with the years; a novice filmmaker, now an old hand; a first-time novelist learning to master his craft; a wounded and wounding husband given the chance to remake his life and forget old wounds; a father blinded by his own youth, clumsiness, and narcissism; then a father again, less selfish at last, open to the gift of childhood and its joys: for each success, each triumph—a mistake, a failure. For every advance, a retreat. Affirmation, negation—each begetting its opposite. At almost every point in his life, doubt and anxiety had gnawed at him. And he had created a very clever front to disguise these constant misgivings.

He had learned how to feign arrogance, insolence, and audacity; how to speak and act with confidence. When quite young, he had created for himself an alternate persona completely unlike his own: at ease with life, nonchalant, seductive, cheerful; above petty jealousies and proof against hypocrisy, rudeness, and vulgarity of soul. With his feet up on the table, but casually elegant, with a princely unselfconsciousness. And to silence all those questions, he had eagerly lived a life of action, travel, creation in all its forms, a frenetic eclecticism. One day a close friend had said to him, "You know why you get involved in so many projects, challenges, performances? You know why? Because you refuse to grow old and think about death."

He had always succeeded in warding off reflection with action. For him, work had been a form of protection. And the second persona had totally eclipsed the first one. They were complementary, in fact, and helped each other out. The more anxiety-ridden and riddled with self-doubt he had become, the more he had drudged, grubbed, sweated, toiled and moiled, pushing himself to do his utmost. And the more interest he had taken in the world: traveling, loving, striving to be open to things, to stand out, to be recognized.

Sometimes he laughed to himself to see the image of this hollow man reflected in other people's eyes. So many labels, so many clichés! He'd heard them all. He had been called everything in the book: an opportunist, a real go-getter, an eager beaver, a young man in a hurry, the most American of our novelists, of our film directors, of our journalists . . . A whole slew of platitudes.

"If only they knew," he'd thought.

But "they" didn't know, and since he didn't want them to know, he kept challenging them—and himself as well.

Pushing Your Luck

NOW HE REMEMBERED one challenge in particular: eight days and nights in a London suburb with Lee, Tom, Mickey, Johnny, and the rest. Johnny had called him in Paris one day.

"I'm recording a whole album. Some of the music is sketched out, but that's it. We'll have all the Beatles' musicians. Not for very long. We've got to take full advantage of them. I haven't a single lyric. You want to do them? You ready to come spend ten days with us, at the studio, going flat out? Writing twelve songs in ten days?"

He'd jumped at the chance. They'd lived like recluses. Smoking, eating, drinking, sleeping very little, sleeping poorly, going from hotel to studio and back again without ever seeing daylight. Lee, with his red sideburns and Oklahoma accent. Tom and Mickey, the composers, close buddies, one with frizzy blond curls, the other sleekly dark-haired, writing simple, easy-to-remember melodies alive with the tempo of the times. He had typed out his lyrics on a portable Olivetti with a blue leather carrying case, the same typewriter he'd used during his heyday as a reporter. He had banged away on it in the silence of the hotel room. There would be a knock at the door. It would be Johnny and his Wilson guitar, full of fun and raring to go.

"Show me what you've got," he would say. "How far along are you? Have you finished 'Sarah'?"

Johnny Hallyday. With his bowlegs, his round shoulders, his half-raffish, half-innocent smile, those striking blue eyes that had seen countless white nights, the incredible body that carried him through everything (so many car crashes and binges with drugs and alcohol that at the time he was known as The Beast), his surprisingly gentle voice, the vulnerability you sensed whenever he talked about his shattered childhood . . . There he would be, standing in the doorway at that late hour like an apparition of one of those rugged Americans whom he had befriended years before in Virginia, Texas, and Colorado. He had the look of a cowboy, the awkward gait of someone who lived on the road, but his voice and the simple truth of him were something else again. He was an artist.

He had a way of picking out the strong phrase, the key words to be set off in the music others wrote for him. He knew how to pinpoint the clumsy line break, the missing beat, the lousy rhyme. He was a performer, but he spurred you on, too, because you felt inspired by who he was, by the kind of life he'd led, by his popularity, and it was easy to write for him. When he turned up at three in the morning to try out new lyrics on his guitar, Johnny became a different person. The subtlety with which he teased out just the right sound, his instinct for salvaging weak spots and filling in gaps made everything go more smoothly. High on laughter and euphoria, we'd scribble our corrections directly on the page in the Olivetti. High on other things, too: beer, tobacco, sleeplessness, and whatever would keep us awake. Then back to the studio we'd go. The instrumentalists had recorded new background music in a variety of styles. The Beast would stand at the mike for a first run-through of the new lyrics.

There were never more than a few words, a few lines, and they would turn into a song. The marathon lasted for days and nights and at the end of it he had gone home, exhausted, to Paris. Leaving Lee, the musicians, and The Beast to complete the project. He'd taken to his bed that same evening with a high fever and a bronchial infection.

The bearded doctor with the Russian accent had pronounced his verdict: "You pushed your luck too far."

TWENTY YEARS LATER—just recently, in other words—did I do it again? "Push my luck too far" when I tried to get the manuscript of my latest novel in on time? Spending night after night dictating, correcting, I had felt feverish, unable to breathe, and I had fallen ill.

I think back to this manuscript: did writing it help bring me to death's door? At this very moment, the book is being typeset by my publisher. A dear friend of mine, a writer, will step in for me and correct the proofs in my place. I learned this from my wife. As I was writing this novel, I began to feel somehow closer to it than I had to any of my previous books. Perhaps because two characters whom

I cared about—Vence, a friend who left this world too soon, and Lumière, a girl of uncanny insight—embodied the precariousness of life, the fragility of our existence. It was a book about youth, about the crazy, deceptive feeling that impelled the narrator and hero (i.e., myself) to seek out risks, love, work, and passion, convinced that at that age, one can triumph over everything—that time is no obstacle, that one lasts for a long while, forever. Later, when the book came out, after my ICU crossing, a friend asked me, "Who dictated this passage to you?"

In the passage in question, the narrator feels and sees his life moving inexorably toward an unknown destiny. Indeed, who had whispered those short paragraphs to me, in which the narrator, at four in the morning on the Boulevard du Montparnasse, watches some young people drive off in convertibles, watches with the sudden conviction that soon they will be nothing more than futility, shadows, and dust. "Who dictated that to you?" When I'd written this passage, late in the spring, my health was beginning to deteriorate. Something within me, inside my body, had started its subterranean work, sapping my strength, undermining me. Had this something— in the ICU, it was referred to as the "unknown bacterium"— prompted me to come up with the words, the phrases, the scenes that smelled so strongly of death? I had dictated the manuscript into a small tape recorder so that it could be retranscribed. These taping sessions had kept me up all night for a week and left me unable to speak, with a swollen larynx, choking sensations, recurrent fevers, and an immune system at low ebb. I felt as though I had come to the end of a series of walls that had crumbled one after the other. And then there had been that constant coughing, and finally the specialist telling me, "I cannot treat you unless you will change your mind and allow yourself to be hospitalized."

Four Take Away One
Equals Three

HOSPITALIZED! At first I had refused.

Everything in me rejected the idea, because I would have to abandon my projects and give in to this illness, and even worse, I would be surrendering myself to a world I had known only as a visitor, the world of sick friends or relatives, of all those failed suicides, or of brutal deaths like Melville's ruptured aneurysm that night: the trip to the hospital, with me out in the hall, bereft, begging the doctors to "revive" him, and them telling me (gesturing toward the huge body of my huge friend, already ashen, drained of his life), "We can't do any more for him, we tried everything."

I hated the idea of being hospitalized.

My wife and daughter had told me, "You have to do it."

Lying on my bed, I had wept like a child in front of them.

"No, I'm not ready!"

There had been a semblance of an argument. The two women, mother and teenager, had put on a show for me.

"If you don't go, we won't speak to you anymore. You'll be on your own."

A few hours later, at the end of my rope, in a panic over my fever, weakness, and the increasing pressure in my chest, I had telephoned the specialist.

"I'm ready."

My wife and daughter had accompanied me. I remember that last car ride. It was a Saturday, a lovely, mild day in late May or early June. I no longer had the strength to talk. The next morning, the bronchoscopy revealed the extent of the disaster, and I was transferred to the ICU.

I think about these events in their proper order. There: I've finally managed to figure out their chronology. Then I start asking myself questions.

"What if that manuscript turns out to be your last book? If you don't make it, will you leave it behind as a posthumous work—and will it be worthy of that special position? Will it take on the aura of a posthumous book? Will it be judged differently? Will people see things in it you had no idea you intended to say?"

But almost immediately I think, "What is so important about all this? Nothing. If you don't wake up, the important thing won't be what you leave behind—or not—of your little literary *oeuvre*, but rather, what will happen to those you love and who love you."

QUERY:

What will happen to the children? What effect will the loss of a parent have on them, at their tender age?

How will their tastes, their laughter, their friendships, their affections, their education, their vocation in life, their health and natural grace be influenced by this unexpected misfortune? Such a devastating event can overwhelm young people, reaching into every last corner of a life transformed forever by sudden grief, leaving them careworn, changing even their body language, their looks and gestures. I was lucky enough to reach adulthood with both my parents still alive. My father was ninety years old when he died, and his death could not have come as a shock or a surprise. My sorrow was tempered by my preparedness, and by my understanding of the inescapable decline of the man I had loved, feared, and respected. Time had given me all the time I needed to accept the inevitable. I still miss him, but the pain of his loss was a gentle one, in a way. But what if something dreadful were to happen in the near future—how would the children bear up under this stunning blow? A tragedy for which nothing has prepared them?

Their mother was not as fortunate as I. She lost her own mother at a very early age, too early for her and for her sisters. Listening to my wife, observing her, living with her, I have realized—imperfectly, superficially—what it means to lose someone so prematurely. Will she know how to and be able to find the strength she will need, even though she has already weathered that earlier trauma? Knowing is one thing, doing is another: I'm not worried that she won't know how to cope with this tragedy. She has had more experience with life's sorrows than I have. But will she be able to? Will she have the heart, day after day, to help her children live without their father? Curiously, the same image of our ritual breakfast scene in the kitchen comes back to me with the precision of a wide-angle photograph: I can see everything in the room, from the farthest corner of the window to the edge of the white counter on which we slice the bread. White walls, white tiled floor, blue kitchen utensils, reproductions of old covers drawn for *The New Yorker*. Colors: blue and emerald green. Without any hazy delirium or pain clouding the image, I can picture the three of them—mother, son, and daughter—each one sitting in front of a bowl of cereal or a cup of tea.

I am not there. Now they are only three. I know that this situation could become permanent, that there might never again be four of us. I'm afraid for them. I fear for Clarisse's bright eyes, for Jean's sunny smile, for that lively, saucy look I never fail to find on Françoise's pert face, no matter what the circumstances. I have always seen a reserve of gaiety behind every other expression of her feelings. An ability to overcome life's despair and transform it into a cheerful approach to living.

They are sitting quietly. Are they listening to the radio? Where's the dog? I see her, on my daughter's lap, with her head tucked under the table.

I tell myself that if I am able to reconstruct such sequences, to wonder about my own questions, it's because my thinking has become clearer. It means I will be able to deal with the ex-tu-ba-tion, in a state of extreme weakness, of course, but also with a certain peace of mind.

To what do I owe this strange equanimity, this tranquility of spirit? I should be in the throes of anxiety. Yet I feel relieved of all fear.

"We're Going to Put You Under Very Deeply"

PERHAPS I HAVE BEEN prepared by my passage through the white tunnel, toward the light.

When I see the door open and Doctor C. come in, giving orders and setting up his equipment with the relaxed and expert air I had noticed during his earlier visits, I am not in the least afraid. My usual paranoia seems to have vanished from both body and mind.

It's morning. Two nurse's aides had come in very early to bathe and weigh me, turn me this way and that, check my IV, take my temperature and my blood pressure, and change the sheets. I think they even washed my face and shaved me.

"Do you know they'll be extubating you at ten o'clock?" one of the aides had asked me. "They already told you that yesterday, didn't they?"

Having no way of telling time, I'd nodded. I would have liked to have said "Hello," "Thank you," to have asked some questions, just as I have wanted to whenever anyone has spoken to me during what must now be a full week of my ICU crossing. My inability to speak has depressed me and made me more aware of my limitations. When will I be able to talk again? Just simply talk! To others, to strangers, to my loved ones. The loss of speech is another deprivation of one's liberty. The ICU is a prison.

I waited. I felt that I wasn't in quite so much pain as before. Was that the result of what they had given me to prepare for the extubation? I hadn't stopped thinking about that white light, the emotion I had experienced, the fleeting sensation of being touched by a loving smile; I couldn't reconstruct the light and the idea of this smile in concrete terms, in words or images, but I remembered that impression, that vision. I told myself that if this didn't go well, if anything went wrong, I would be carried irrevocably to the "other side," where the white tunnel and the light would most likely be waiting for me again. All this meant that I should be at peace and unafraid. It was the best way, the only way to approach this major turning point, the last one before death. And then I thought about my son, the little boy who would be going off to school this morning knowing that his father would be "extubated." And about my teenage daughter, whose mother had probably told her the same news.

"They're going to free Papa from the machine this morning."

She had doubtless told them both the same thing, at the same time, over their chocolate breakfast cereal. Of course she had been determined not to show the slightest apprehension. Had she really spoken the words I'd imagined?

"They're going to free Papa."

The word *papa* made me think about my father and my group of visitors. In the end, they had never returned to the room to urge me, "Come on! What are you waiting for? Join us!"

They had given up on me and dropped their invitation. I decided this was a sign. Doctor C. had entered the room. So it had to be ten o'clock in the morning.

DOCTOR C. is very well organized.

I watch everything he does, I hear every word he says, as though I were in a theater. Observing how he assigns tasks to the nurse's aides, who listen respectfully, I decide that he's a superb professional. You can always tell a pro. At the head of a team or the wheel of a car, in the printing plant of a newspaper, behind a camera or a microphone, you recognize the pro by an economy of movement, the impression that everything has already been rehearsed, thought over, tried out. And there is that kind of gentle firmness in the orders given—an authority that doesn't need to be authoritarian to make itself understood. It reassures you. It neutralizes your reluctance and resistance. The pro does his job, the way a cabinetmaker constructs his chair.

I who have lost all memory, except for fragments here and there, I who have been reduced to reciting a few random verses of poetry day and night in order to survive, I suddenly hear, at the sight of Doctor C. at work, a text by Charles Péguy, read in my father's voice, the way he used to do during my childhood.

... The rung of a chair had to be well made. That was understood. That was paramount. It did not have to be well made for the wages, for the boss or for the connoisseurs, or for the boss's clients. It had to be well made for itself, in itself, of itself, in its very being. A healthy tradition, observed since time immemorial. History, integrity, honor demanded that this chair rung be well made. Every unseen part of the chair was just as perfectly made as the parts that could be seen. This is the very guiding principle of cathedrals.

I remember the slightly incantatory tone with which my father read us this text as he walked up and down the large family dining room. I remember how Péguy's repetitive lyricism drummed that truth into us, that priestly duty: the chair rung had to be well made. And now, lying here with my arms tied down, intubated, full of cortisone and antibiotics, enfeebled, after crossing the darkness and then the light, I watch Doctor C. getting ready to perform the most important act of my life with the feeling that he is a craftsman who abides by the tenets of integrity and self-respect invoked by Charles Péguy. In what I have tried to accomplish, in the exercise of all the professions I have taken on "for fear of growing old," as my friend had told me, I have been greatly influenced by this text from my earliest childhood. I watch Doctor C.—patient, methodical, concentrating on his craft—with the certainty that he belongs to that same brotherhood praised by Péguy, and I tell myself that there is a secret bond between this Doctor C., whom I do not know, and my father, who has been dead now for many a year and who already be-

longed to a bygone time. The bond between Doctor C. and my father comes from something that no one dares mention nowadays:
it's called "honor."

ON A LITTLE TABLE at the head of my bed, Doctor C. sets
out a kind of small metal case from which he draws objects I
cannot identify. A young woman is with him, and I feel that I
have seen her before, here, in the hospital. Although no one in
the room has mentioned her name, it suddenly comes to me:
Lisyane. That's it, her name is definitely Lisyane. She has red
hair and light green eyes, and I've already seen these two colors—red, light green—bending over me.

"Do you recognize me?" she asks. "I'm the one who anesthetized
you for your first bronchoscopy."

So she was present at the initial stage, and now I meet her again
for what should lead to my departure from the ICU—if all goes well.
A surgical mask really sets off a person's eyes, and Lisyane's seem
to speak to me as I listen to her words.

"I'm going to give you something that will put you under very
briefly—because the extubation won't take long at all—but very
deeply."

I smile to myself at this last phrase. Can they send me under any
more deeply than I have already gone, and more than once? Fine—
let's plumb the depths! I've been there. I know what it's like.

Soon the faces of Doctor C. and Lisyane melt away, and this time, without me realizing it. It all happens quite quickly, and I must have gone so "deep" that to this day, I have no memory of the abyss into which the anesthesiologist with the light green eyes so skillfully plunged me. As I write these lines, I can think back to every moment of my crossing, but that particular voyage into the deep sends up no image, no terror, no darkness, no light. Complete obliteration of everything.

I remember only my awakening and what it meant.

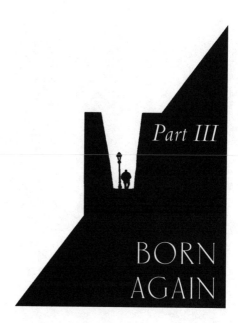

Part III

BORN
AGAIN

A Blank Parchment

SILENCE. And faint sounds, benign ones, with no intent to cause harm. Everyday sounds.

The BOOM-BOOM-RAT-TA-TAM is gone.

The respirator is gone. The alarm bell is gone. The hoarse breathing is gone.

The tube is gone. The permanent threat I had felt hanging heavily in the room, above and all around me, is gone.

That hot, thick, black river flooding my lungs is gone. There is cool air, as crisp and bracing as the morning breeze in a dewy glade. I breathe this air through open nostrils, down an unclogged, unobstructed throat, into a clear chest. I'm not choking anymore. My hacking cough is gone. The foreign element that had taken me over has left my territory. I am no longer occupied by enemy forces.

The air I breathe in freely through my mouth is breathed out again. I inhale and exhale. I feel myself come back to life.

THE ROOM I'M IN, the bed where I'm lying, the ceiling I see above me are the same as those I left a half-hour ago. Still, everything has changed. The proportions are normal, real. I've lost that impression of things that seemed skewed, of enlarged and distorted dimensions, fantastically empty and dark at times, and at others, terribly narrow and constricting. I feel that I might be able to speak. I don't dare try yet, but I sense the words waiting at the back of my throat and palate. A profound feeling of satisfaction slowly comes over me. I'm not a prisoner anymore! This means that they succeeded, I'm extubated. I have returned from the other side, to this one here. I am back among the living. Then my mind and body thrill to a feeling of relief and clarity. Of utter weakness, true, but also lucidity and transparence. Well-being. Like a green-and-yellow scent, the smell of flowers and leaves. Odors, aromas! I had forgotten what a smell is like. It has been so long since I've smelled anything.

I'm awake. I feel a spray on my face. I'm familiar with this system: a little bottle with a tube leading to a small plastic object suspended above your nose sends you a smoky vapor, a soothing mist of Soludecadron to inhale. After falling asleep again once or twice, I will wake up completely, and then all sorts of extraordinary things will happen. In the hours following the extubation, I will see unrolling before me a kind of blank parchment on which messages will appear. I will see what I should say, do, write, plan, and accomplish. How I should approach life, as I return to it.

During this period—I have no way of knowing how long it

lasts—I will feel that the chaos I have experienced until now is dissipating, that my thoughts and memories are falling back into place. It's a straightening-up operation, a rearranging and redistribution of ideas and feelings. My first thought is, "I'm okay. I'm weak, but I'm alive. I'm alive!"

And then, right away, in an orderly sequence that proceeds as swiftly as if it were computerized, the things I should do come to mind: I must tell everyone to whom I haven't said this often enough that I love them, and tell them why; I must apologize and offer explanations for having recently done this or that thing that may have hurt or worried anyone; I must write or produce such and such a book, program, article. I see the things I must work for scrolling before my eyes. I see scenarios, titles, themes, and characters. Then I see an outline of my activities for the next five years. But at the same time, I also see the list of all those things I have left undone in word and deed, all that unfinished business I would have regretted—if the worst had happened—in the very second before my death. People say, "I've regretted it all my life." They should say, "I'd have regretted it all my death!"

I WILL HAVE TO undo and then redo whatever I have said or done out of pride, narcissism, egotism, impatience, and negativism; redo everything without letting my ego become involved in it in any way. And I must replace pride with a little modesty, narcissism with a little personal detachment, egotism with a little generosity, impatience with a little serenity, and negativism with a little optimism. And I think it will be easy. Really, even too easy!

As soon as I'm up to it, I will have to see those professional colleagues with whom I have worked in the same offices for almost ten years so that I can speak to them, not about what they decided while I was gone, and how things went, and who did what, or who said what, but about what I think of them and how much I appreciate what they are, who they are. And I must ask them about themselves, their health, their families, their cares and anxieties. Above all, I should pay attention to Françoise, who must have had a wretched time of it, not eating or sleeping properly, getting no rest, probably dealing with everything herself, coping and bearing up, taking care of our home, the children, and her professional life, and doubtless managing everyone else's grief and activity as well. Only now am I beginning to realize how she had to screen and organize, evaluate and delegate calls, visits, messages, tasks—and how, surrounded by the urgent queries of my entire family, she must have been at the center of this play, the last act of which has yet to be written. I will have to pay attention to her and for her: after such a grueling experience, a thread can sometimes be broken, and a crystal shattered.

Then I must speak more—and more from the heart—to my children and to my friends. I who thought I knew how to speak, how to explain, show, instruct, write, how to "communicate"—that modern expression I reject the instant I think of it—I discover that I haven't quite figured out how to tell the truth, speak with sincerity, give things we take for granted their due.

"Just imagine," I tell myself, "if you hadn't made it through this, if you'd stayed down in the black hole. You would have left only unfinished, faulty things behind. Now you've been given a second chance, a chance to be a bit better than you were before. To be more straightforward, loving, genuine."

Then this next thought occurs to me.

"You must do better with your second chance at life."

And I fall asleep without having been able to say a single word yet. I fall asleep hoping that I am truly safe at last.

34

Knowing How to Put Things in Perspective

THE THING IS, you find it hard to believe.

Sleep plays tricks on you. Even though you are no longer imprisoned by the respirator, there are lingering aftereffects from the sedatives. The sea doesn't withdraw in a single wave, and neither does horror.

And so the big black nightmare of orange shapes oozing toward you and little top-men in cricket caps—all that shows up again, in bits and pieces, fits and starts. When it does, you look for the light and open your eyes.

Reality chases it away. Whatever you see, out in the hallway, on the other side of the glass panels, or bustling around the bed in your room—all this reassures you and confirms the feeling you had when you awoke: everything is breathing. You are aware of this true mystery, the ordinary passage of air through your body, only because it was almost taken from you. Your first natural breaths (drawn without the help of the nebulizer, which has been removed so that your respiration can return to normal) resemble the discovery of a new country where everything is different, welcoming, pleasant. It's fresh, clean, lovely, pristine. It's the wind rustling the blue trees in Colorado. I understand why I thought about them so much: it was the lack of air, wind, sky, and freedom that made me dream of those wide open spaces.

It's a primal feeling. It goes beyond the most intoxicating experience of one's first love, first symphony, first poetic or artistic emotion, first creative triumph, first pride at having done something well. It exceeds the very definition of excess. You are experiencing a unique moment, and at the same time, to counterbalance this glow of exaltation, you feel something else, something just as strong: a great humility.

"This is nothing," you realize. "Try to put things in perspective. Imagine the past, present, and future sufferings of others; the trials and agonies of patients with cancer, with AIDS; the tribulations of those whose hearts are failing and who undergo triple or quadruple bypasses; the martyrdom of those stricken with paralysis, with diseases of the brain, the glands, the blood. Think of other people. You haven't lived through anything as tragic as that, after all."

It dawns on me that other men and women have been in this bed, in this room that I can describe down to the last banal detail, and for these patients, the voyage has been fearsome indeed. A voyage of no return. I can easily imagine it, with the special insight born of experience. Gazing without anguish at the ceiling overhead, I wonder: How many brothers and sisters in pain stared up at it just before dying? Then, my humble awareness that I have come close to nothingness, that I am only one case lost among the boundless and universal population of those who suffer, brings a sort of calm to the exaltation of my return. A new refusal of the ego: from now on, the great Me is nothing more than little me.

And then, at the same time, comes the irresistible longing to see, to touch, to hear other people. It's a hunger, a thirst. As the hours and days go by, in this same room where I have seen the unseen, and known the unknown, my family and friends will be coming to see me, and I will be seeing them with new eyes.

35

The Boasty Boy's Song

THE FIRST VISIT is from Françoise, not long after the extubation. She's wearing the usual obligatory gauze mask, but I can see the smile behind it. Since I cannot speak yet, I write on the plastic slate.

I write like a madman, my hand racing along too fast. I try to express the relief and gratitude I feel at seeing her. My words are for her and our children. I see a gleam of happiness in her hazel-green eyes. There is not a trace of fear in that lovely, beaming face.

I'm hard at work: writing, writing. The slate is full, front and back. I hand it to her. She reads, replies with tender gestures; the gauze mask somewhat muffles her answers, but I understand the faintest intonations of that carefully modulated voice. It's as if the great upheaval I have been through has given me the curious ability to interpret the unspoken language of the eyes and body more clearly, to read more deeply into silences. On the slate she has wiped clean, since I signaled that I hadn't finished and still had so many things to say, I ask her to tell me about herself—there has been enough worrying about me!—to tell me if she's all right. I beg her to forget about me for just one second. She doesn't say much in reply, taking care to let me pour out this excess of emotion, to let this inevitable, indispensable liberation run its course.

She hands me a pocket-sized notebook with a black cover, a tiny pencil tucked into a thin leather sheath lying along the cut edge of the pad, and an elastic band that fits around the cover to keep the notebook closed.

"You'll have many things to write down in the days ahead."

I try to write what I hope is a real expression of love that a man can say to a woman, and a woman to a man.

"I love you for what you are. Because you are."

I keep writing.

"I can't live without you."

I keep writing.

"Talk to me about yourself."

She replies quietly that she's "fine." And that the children will be coming very soon.

THEY HAD ALREADY been there, actually, although I only learned this later.

In my pain and delirium, however, I hadn't been aware of them. Once, opening my eyes to escape the cackling grimaces of the little top-men, I had indeed thought I'd seen my daughter (with her long hair and her familiar way of standing—things a father would know so well) outside the glass-paneled door to my room, and I'd also thought I'd seen her recoil in revulsion and fear. I had thought, "She's horrified by what she sees of me, she's leaving." It didn't happen like that, naturally, and we will gradually realize that nothing of what I was able to see "happened like that."

But she really did come, since she was old enough to be allowed into the ICU. She had seen a man stuffed with tubes, lying on a bed. And she has never told me what her reaction was. There had been a problem with the little boy, though, because he was too young. Thanks to the doctor's thoughtfulness, he had been allowed into a small inner courtyard on a level with the window of my room. I hadn't noticed him, but it had been a good thing to do, as it was important to show him that his father truly was there.

Now that I am able to send him real signs of life, he has come back to the same little courtyard. His mother has arranged everything so that he can see for himself that I'm "free," that "Papa's out of danger."

I can see him clearly through the glass. I can even make out his face. There is a kind of plastic window he could speak through, but he'd rather not. Is he too shy to say anything? There are people with him: a nurse, his mother. He leans forward and smiles. Then I make all kinds of gestures and signs. A frenetic "V for Victory" with each hand, the way he used to do when he was very small. Then, a thumb's-up to show that I've won, everything's okay. Next I go through a series of hand movements: potato-fists, hands wide open, fingers signaling numbers—it's "The Boasty Boy's Song," known only to the two of us, one of the innumerable secrets shared by a father and son. He's the "boasty boy," and the song we made up together is just the list of the blows you fake when pretending to fight: "a poke in the nose" (one finger), "four wallops" (four fingers), "three biffs" (three fingers), "and twenty-five thwacks" (all five fingers on both hands flashed twice, then all five on a single hand once, making twenty-five). No gestures accompany the rest of the ritual.

>   That makes many a sly ploy
>   For a sweet little boasty boy.

But I manage to act out the end of our song as well, pointing my index finger at him, my boasty boy.

He smiles at my performance. Can he tell, through the window, that I'm smiling, too? We're a pair of lone Indians who have recognized each other in the darkness out on the plains, and we've exchanged our secret signs. Complicity, affection, inner jubilation. After many waves good-bye, the little boy leaves.

"You're lucky, you're lucky, you're lucky . . ."

Like locomotive wheels, like pistons pumping rhythmically up and down, I hear these words humming along, over and over, subliminally. Because the aftereffects of the anesthesia sometimes cause me to lose consciousness for a little while.

Four Steps for Dealing with Pain

IT DOESN'T LAST: soon I am perfectly lucid again, back in my room with its furnishings, the nurses, the daylight, and a thought that comes whirling back to me: the others. Those who have occupied this room, and those who will do so in the future.

"You didn't have such a bad time of it," I reflect. "There are men and women who have been through repeated stays in an ICU, who have been anesthetized and operated on dozens of times. Doctors have examined, handled, sliced up, mangled, biopsied, removed, and replaced their livers, hearts, lungs, bladders, pancreases. They know these empty walls better than anyone, and these blue or yellow ceilings, these air vents, this hospital furniture, this stark universe, and their arms are almost—how shall I put it?—used to being stabbed for the IV drip and the blood draws. They have weathered more pain and more acceptance of this pain and more knowledge of this pain than you will have acquired in your stay here. Because, after all, the crossing was a short one, so you've no reason to complain."

And I'm not complaining, either.

This is another surprising aspect of the return to life: no complaints. No desire, no need to call the world to witness what one has seen and been through. I who quaked at the slightest scratch, the supersensitive hypochondriac who delighted in his "boo-boos" like a frail child, who never really acted like anything but a spoiled crybaby clamoring for care and attention even during the most ordinary illness—I have stopped whining.

A NEW PRINCIPLE to be added to my list: There are four steps to dealing with pain. First of all, you must acknowledge it. Secondly, if you've acknowledged it, you must accept it. Thirdly, since you've accepted it, you can try to break free of it. Fourthly, and lastly, you are therefore capable of rising above it, since you know it so well.

From now on I have a pain standard, like the "shit detector" Hemingway said he used to unmask imposters and frauds. This pain standard, this inner compass that allows the traveler to stay on course, will help me put all other pain into perspective. Whenever someone draws a little blood from me (they will have to make sure I continue to improve, after all), or moves me around in the bed, or when they take out the catheter and then after that, when I pee razor blades for weeks because I just happen to have picked up a severe and tenacious infection (the classic souvenir of a stay in the ICU), all my body will have to say to me, right before the pain hits, is: "This is nothing. Think about what you've experienced, and tell yourself that what you're going through is nothing. It's a trifle compared with what has already happened to you."

When you have suffered that much, you don't suffer anymore. I greet the nurse's aides with the smile of someone who knows. I close my eyes, they find the vein, I haven't felt a thing. It isn't important. When you have been that afraid, you can't be afraid anymore. And so, after this awakening, I am certain of one thing: although I barely escaped death and was frightened by it, although I looked death in the face and felt its cold hand and pushed it away—now that I know, I will no longer be afraid. It isn't that I was afraid of death before, but I wanted to ignore it in spite of having brushed up against it as we all do. Each time death struck around or near me (wars, accidents, natural causes, hospitals, friends, relatives, strangers), each time I was a spectator, witness, or even an accompanist of death, I completely rejected death. I refused to hear its message of warning.

"I am here: I can arrive at any moment. Don't forget that I am yours, that you are mine. We belong to each other. Do not forget that."

I won't ever forget that again—but it doesn't frighten me anymore.

37

Where Has Karen Gone?

THE NURSES CAN TELL that I know. We don't talk about it, but I see it in their eyes, in their attitude. I don't know anything about them. I needed them, I loved and sometimes hated them, but I know nothing about them and want very much to talk to them.

Because, at last, I can talk. My lips, my mouth, my throat have been set free. The nebulizer treatment is administered only at specific times now, so aside from that, my face is free. Of course, my arms are still encumbered with a few wires, and the pulse oximeter remains on my fingertip, but they have removed the Velcro restraints from the metal bed rails since there is no reason for me to try to rip out tubes that have disappeared. On my palate and around my mouth, however, I can still feel the tube and its little ties, and I think I hear the numbing noise of the machine with which I was supposed to "work."

As a matter of fact, the first words I hear myself say out loud are, "The machine and the tubes. The tubes and the machine."

As if to exorcize them, to expel them from my body's memory. I had thought I was alone in the room, but a voice replies, "What did you say?"

It's one of the nurses, Bénédicte, the one from whom I expected so much in my moments of deepest despair, the one who personified aid, the helping hand of life. I say her name in praise and gratitude, several times. She comes over to me.

"So," she asks me, patting my forearm, "are you going to be okay now? We won't have much time to talk together, you know, before you leave the ICU. I've got other patients who aren't well at all."

"I must have been a lot of trouble," I reply. "I probably bothered you every night and I pushed the call button way too many times for you to come 'suction' me."

She shakes her head, a gesture that has become so familiar to me, a mixture of brusque good nature and common sense, but also an expression of her great experience with illness, pain, and death, which gives her that unspoken edge over so many others, the superiority of one who knows and who no longer even has the desire, need, or time to talk about it. That shake of her head is the equivalent of the old Oriental saying: "He who knows does not speak; he who speaks does not know."

"Not at all," she says in the end, still working away. "You didn't push the call button any more often than others do."

SHE HAS BEEN HERE in the ICU for more than two years. She's the strongest, the most respected, and the most stubborn, too, of all the nurses. One of the veterans. She is aware that she will eventually wind up with "ICU burnout," yet at the same time, she's not satisfied anywhere but in this atmosphere, this constant tension, these extreme conditions, where lives are on the line, and she must cope with danger and her patients' desperate need for her competence. She's single, and commutes to the hospital all the way from Yvelines. Her parents were born in Touraine—I don't know why I thought her background was Corsican. She and another nurse who has only recently been assigned to the ICU are thinking about going to Africa, to Rwanda, to one of those refugee camps where one is even more in the thick of pain and suffering, where one must push oneself even harder, "to the limit," she says. As if her experience in the ICU of a big Parisian hospital, far from making her tire of the fight against death, were instead giving her extra enthusiasm for things she doesn't mention (through modesty, pride, or a simple refusal to use these words, which she certainly knows) and which we call charity, communion, love, self-abnegation.

Her friend has just come into the room. They will be working as a team for the next eight hours. The young woman is a light-skinned Guadeloupean with short hair, a serene face, and a calm, judicious way of speaking. When she comes over to clean my mouth, I recognize her, no doubt about it. Then I tell her how touched I had been by her patience and courtesy when I was coughing, imprisoned by tubes, wrestling with my inability to follow her instructions or reply to her request repeated with such gentle insistence: "I wish to reach your palate."

She smiles at that. We talk. I try to learn something about her, about her life. She is the mother of a little girl; the father no longer lives with them. She has just completed a long stretch as a nurse in a psychiatric ward. When I question her a bit too quickly or too closely, the young woman lowers a polite curtain of silence and discretion; now that I can talk again, I'm probably talking too much, probing too clumsily, too eagerly, in my desire to get to know one of these women who have been so important to me. Her silence means the same thing as when Bénédicte shook her head a little while ago.

"Yes, yes, of course, you love us and you're passionately interested in us and that's just fine, and it's very kind, and it's even quite nice because it doesn't happen all that often—but it won't last. You'll soon be discharged from the ICU, within the next forty-eight hours, and you'll be moved into a room on a floor in the pulmonary building, and you'll be in the care of other nurses and nurse's aides, and you'll forget us. Yes, yes, during your Night Crossing, you needed us, naturally, and you needed us so much that you became unusually attached to us, and we've done our best to help you, but you'll be leaving us and we'll be staying here, traffic police at the crossroads of the capital of pain, in this ICU that is both a prison where we are the guards, and a rescue center where we are ministering angels. Your bed will be occupied by a man or woman to whom we will have to give the same extreme attention, the same vigilance, the same compassion, the same stern and caring words, and with them, too, there will be no room for mistakes. And so we are not going to reveal to you after all the secret of our lives, loves, weaknesses, hopes, and failures, just because you're burning with human curiosity and questioning us with that indiscretion we've come to recognize in those who have returned from so far away, from such great solitude."

I understood the nurses perfectly, even though they never made this speech. I know better now how to respect someone's silence or mute shake of the head. I feel that I know better how to be with other people, how to get along with them, whoever they are. For instance, I'm better at listening when Florence, the Guadeloupean, talks to me about my wife or my older daughters. And about how she had seen that one of them seemed to be almost unconsciously "at prayer," while another was all energy and willpower, and the third, all quiet devotion and courage.

BÉNÉDICTE AND FLORENCE leave me alone. For a moment, there is no one at the nurse's work counter. Will I also see Karen the Korean again, I wonder? Venomous Karen? Karen who used to scare me so much in her green scrubs when I saw her from the back, at night, as she was preparing her medications and chattering away to her little friend in that bitchy voice about her screwed-up love life—scared me enough to make me fear the two of them were going to murder me . . . Where has Karen gone?

38

On the Cretinization
of the World

THE SPECIALIST, DOCTOR D., seems relieved and satisfied to see me "on the right track."

In his slightly husky voice, he explains the future stages of my "discharge plan" to me: a little while longer in the ICU, then a few weeks in a room here in the hospital, so that I can regain my strength and the weight I lost, but also and particularly so that they can make sure the treatment they have chosen is having its full effect.

"You had us worried," he tells me. "I must admit, we were rather at a loss for a few days. But we kept searching. You know, that's the only truth in medicine: we're searching. We think we know, but we're often wrong and we search on. It's the lab that gave us the answer. I confess I even consulted a few colleagues. I'm not embarrassed to tell you. We really hunted around. Don't believe all that fancy stuff you hear about medicine: we know everything—and nothing. I'm not going to release you until we're sure you're out of the woods. This could take a little more time, and you'll have to allow us to take this time."

He's wearing an almost apologetic expression; it was he who had urged me to enter this hospital in the first place and whose advice I had refused to follow, on the grounds that I didn't have the time. He was the one to whom I had explained, a few weeks ago, about my life, the radio and TV, the books, responsibilities, appointments, contracts, meetings, schedules—and he was the one who had listened, respectful of the "importance" of my duties. Today I feel almost ashamed of this, and almost like laughing about it.

"I'll give you all the time you like," I tell him. "It's not important, I've got all the time in the world. My notion of time has changed completely from what it was before. I'm in absolutely no hurry."

He looks at me, smiling in disbelief.

"Listen," I say, "believe me, that comedy is over."

THE COMEDY OF TIME. I had played my part in it like everyone else, perhaps better and more intensely than others of my generation. The comedy of the "busy man," older brother to that up-and-comer, the "young man in a hurry." With a single sentence, a single aerosol-free breath in the ICU room stripped of its respirator, beneath the at first amused, then incredulous, and finally persuaded eye of Doctor D. (persuaded because he knows you do not lie after going through such an ordeal and when you are facing a man who understands what you have been through), this particular comedy (I have others) simply self-destructs. I feel naked, real, more natural than I have ever been able to be. Obstacles just melt away.

On top of this insight into the comedy I've been playing comes a sensation of clairvoyance, like the feeling I had earlier when I'd seemed to see everything that I ought to say and do in the future written out before my eyes.

Clairvoyance and lightness. In this same moment, I lightly cast off certain habits. The prating and ranting of men, their idle chatter—what does it mean? It's nothing. Montaigne had said so, but I hadn't always been listening: "The greatest prince in the world never sits but on his ass." I had never claimed to be a prince, but I had often thought I was seated a bit higher than on my ass. I can see myself again, relaxed and pretending to smile at such things, but privately quite pleased to be receiving awards and medals, honors and prizes. Someone says nice things about me in front of me, in public; I say nice things about the person who talked about me. There are flashbulbs popping, glittering chandeliers, microphones, cameras, ministers, and stars. Everyone applauds. The parquet floor of the majestic reception room in the elegant mansion at the prestigious address seems to float beneath my feet. I'm in heaven, I'm smiling, shaking hands, trading air kisses—oh, my God, I'm so important!

Oh, my God, it's so unimportant!

"Considering all the medications you took," Doctor D. tells me, "I'm surprised to find you so clear-headed."

"What medications?"

"You were given lots of sedatives and painkillers. Don't forget that you were anesthetized twice in one week. Certain drugs confuse and erase one's sense of time. Something that actually lasts for two seconds may seem to you to go on for hours."

I think back to the two tunnels: the black one, then the white. I remember the top-men in cricket caps. The concert of stupefying tropical sounds that invaded my mind to the rhythm of the respirator.

"Usually," he continues, "people come out of that sort of thing in a real fog, and certainly not with the clarity of mind I see in you. You have undergone a disturbing, profoundly unsettling experience. It's as though it has brought you, now, to this astonishing lucidity. It's most unusual."

Certain medications, he said. Are they the explanation for some of my visions? Did they liberate something in my subconscious—or else create something that simply wasn't me? I don't question him. Instead I feel this need to take his hand and shake it earnestly. I will be feeling these affectionate impulses, these longings for physical contact, in the presence of all those I'll be seeing again in the days that follow. I blurt out what's on my mind.

"You belong to an extraordinary profession, you deal with concrete reality. Whereas we, those who work in the media—we work at the representation of this life, this reality. And some of us are even involved with its presentation—we are presenters. Does it mean we're just presenting life, as though it were on display in a store window? Small-scale stuff! You people, you live life. You touch it, you save it, you watch over it throughout your professional lives. You're at the very core of things. And when I say you, I'm talking about you as a specialist as well as your anesthesiologists, your ENTs, your nurses. Oh, our trade isn't any more empty or frivolous than other occupations, but when we compare it to yours, we feel useless, superfluous. And sometimes I tell myself that all I've done is round up words, arrange pictures. You, you touch the body, the blood, the heart and lungs, you're in contact with the ultimate enigma. It's not surprising that those of your profession who write should have felt compelled to address the question of faith, of spirituality."

I can't stop talking.

"I see so many clowns in the circles where I move, so many imposters and nonentities. There's talent, true, and creation, passion, and grace. And laughter! But sometimes we meet with too much that's neither here nor there. Whereas you're at the heart of the matter. You're in real life."

"Perhaps," he replies. "But you're probably laboring under a few illusions. Our world isn't free of falsity, hypocrisy, pretense, vanity, megalomania. It's true that we are the healers. It's true that we do, sometimes, succeed in healing. Maybe we know how we do it, but I'm not sure that we know why. There's a mystery to healing."

"Intelligent cretins would say that, faced with this mystery, you are deeply involved in the 'deconstruction of rationality.'"

He bursts out laughing. "Intelligent cretins?"

"Yes, there can be an imbecility in intelligence—the stupidity that trusts only in rationality. And then, what I've just learned leads me to foresee, I'm not too sure why, the cretinization of our present world. Ever since the extubation, that word has been constantly on my lips. Was it something I saw during my crossing? Is that what those top-men were? We live in a civilization bombarded with stultifying sounds and images. The world grows more stupid at an ever faster rate, at the speed of flickering images. I feel that quite deeply at this very moment, while I'm talking to you. I tell myself that I ought to be more careful about shielding my children from mass communications, from the ways in which our culture fails them. Are we raising them correctly? Haven't we abandoned our duty to explain things to them, to nourish them aesthetically? Do we give education all the importance it should have?"

Doctor D. looks at the notebook lying on the bedside table.

"I see you're already taking notes," he says. "You have to rest, too. The nurse's log seems to indicate that you're not sleeping much."

It's true, I cannot stay asleep for more than a little while at a time. I'm too excited. I rest in short stretches. A dreamless sleep, an unfathomable sleep.

And when I wake up, I discover a new face.

In Which We Meet Doctor T.

HE'S A STRANGER, wearing the same white coat as the other doctors or interns. Who is he? What is he doing here?

He must be about forty; he has the face of a helicopter pilot, an expedition leader, or a single-handed sailor. The look of a man who loves the outdoors, with crinkles around his sparkling eyes, a frank and ready smile, an unaffected voice, as gentle and candid as that of a friend. But a friend whom I've never met before. Yet I feel an immediate liking for him.

"I'm Doctor T., Jean-Pierre T.," he tells me. "Some mutual acquaintances introduced me to your wife, and she has brought me to you. I'm not connected with this hospital, but I know some people here and I was able to keep informed about your illness, enough to be of assistance to your family, talking to them, listening, reassuring them. I see you're doing well. Sergio sends you a kiss; I took care of him during his passage around Cape Horn, the same one you've just made."

He leans down and kisses my forehead.

During the following weeks, he will occasionally stop by my room, unannounced, to see how my "return from Cape Horn" is coming along, and to share with me his thoughts about pain, a phenomenon that seems to fascinate him. That's how I will get to know him, because I had no need to get to love him—I was drawn to him that very first time we met, when he spoke to me at my bedside. I'd felt as though I already knew him, that he was a familiar companion.

He is completely accessible and has the ability to put you at your ease. Later—several months later—he will place his time and knowledge at the service of the French president, in the last stages of his fatal illness. But right now, Doctor T. seems almost like a guardian angel. He has the protective kindness of an angel, a constant willingness to respond to your appeals. Like a guardian, he is experienced, confident, reliable. A man you would like to have at your side in a tough spot.

DOCTOR T.'S MENTION of Sergio and the "rounding of Cape Horn" intrigued me right away. I managed to get Sergio to come see me that very day. Apart from my own family, he was the person I wanted to see first of all. Why Sergio, who doesn't really belong to that network of friends and colleagues with whom I come into contact every day? Because a year earlier, he had almost lost his face, his limbs, and even his life in a car accident. Week after week, he had struggled against death. Patiently, skillfully, his medical team had put him back together. Whenever we met (for lunch every few months), I'd been curious about that: the crossing, the turning point, the trip out and home. But I hadn't been able to worm anything explicit out of him. He would put me off, saying, "Let's talk about something else." Or, "You can't understand unless you've been through it yourself."

And here he is, smiling amiably. We'll have this in common from now on. Of course, the severity and duration of the pain we each experienced were different, and I imagine that of the two of us, he was the one who suffered the most, even though he conceded, once we had compared notes, that I had probably taken more of a psychological beating. He hadn't seen either the white tunnel or the black abyss. No matter: we could talk over our two voyages as accomplices, initiates. He hadn't seen the "other side," because he'd been too frantic, too mentally focused on the single desperate idea of surviving. But the voyages resembled one another in this, at least: we had returned. And we could laugh about it. I'm not sure that our tête-à-tête was entirely free of a kind of simplistic pride, that form of innocent vanity seen in those privileged enough to have lived through a remarkable event. You might also call it a feeling of fraternity.

He brings me news of the "village" to which we both belong in Paris, where each profession hums along in a community brimming with all sorts of stories, anecdotes, intrigues, and revelations. Our journalistic village consists of multiple networks—in politics, the arts, business, the economy—and the gossip about men and women there is no more or less salacious, astonishing, or banal than in the other villages that make up our city. Sergio announces the beginning of the end for a notorious faker whose career has been flawless until now, tells me of the risky romantic involvements of a brash young woman who is a newcomer to our profession, and gives me his opinion of the chances of an as-yet-undeclared candidate for the presidency of the Republic, whom everyone now considers a sure winner. I begin to tire. He stops.

"You're not the least bit interested in what I'm saying, are you?"

"Nope," I tell him. "You're right."

"Take care of yourself," he says as he leaves. "All your life from now on, everything, is a lucky bonus. Be happy—you've rounded Cape Horn. And take your time before you start showing an interest in village affairs again."

"If I ever do," I reply.

I look at his face one last time. The way I see him has changed. Before, when I looked at Sergio, I saw the charmer, the man of talent and influence, the pro who was a bit of a cynic as well as a friend. I feel that I don't see people quite the same way I used to. We all wear masks, more or less. My crossing seems to have given me, perhaps only for the time being, the ability to see more clearly behind the mask. I see people plain and undisguised. Doubtless because I myself have been stripped bare. In Sergio, as he leaves me, I see the child who still lives within him. I see the kindness and goodness that outweigh the ambition and craving for power; I see his vulnerability more than his strength. I even see the dead man he might have been.

40

"I Know Not What Power"

ROUNDING CAPE HORN.

This metaphor turned up often enough that, while I was writing this account, I decided to question a sailor who had made that great voyage. When I reread the notes I took during our telephone conversation, I thought that they applied quite well to my own ICU crossing.

"In the first place," the sailor told me, "out there—near the South Pole, Cape Horn—you know that when you set out, you're not sure of coming back. You're completely alone. No one can come help you. You're alone in the world. You're like Adam. In twenty-nine days at sea, I must have seen the sun just once. The waves were meeting like trains crashing into one another: trains of waves on the left running into trains of waves from the right. It was hellish. You can't navigate. You know about the fears of childhood and the terrors of a grown man, but this is the abject panic of a child of eight. And in fact, you are eight years old.

You're in constant danger for a month, which means that the slightest incident becomes an accident, and the slightest accident becomes fatal. Because everything is augmented, increased, magnified. There is nobody out there where you are, nobody can come rescue you, and to pull through, you need more than the resources of your body, your energy, and the stoutness of your boat; what you can do and what you know how to do—they aren't enough, either. You also need some fairy dust."

"Luck?"

"Of course. And when you return from the Horn, you come back to life. You leave the world of death behind. You're happy, you've broadened your horizons. You see life in a whole new way. You want and need to love the people you love even more than before. And you're suddenly filled with all these needs: to see people you haven't seen for a long while, to change things, adjust your aim, pay attention to a part of yourself you've never taken the time to deal with before. Because you've been through a decisive moment."

"Thanks, Olivier, that fits pretty well. It's almost the same. Thanks."

There was one difference, after all, when I reread my notes, and when Olivier had told me, "You're completely alone," he had unwittingly pointed it out: I wasn't alone. I thought I was, but I wasn't. If I rounded Cape Horn, if I came back toward the sun, if I sailed into the Pacific Ocean, it's not only because my mind and body fought back, it's also because there were men and women who helped me get through this "decisive moment." I was fortunate. I had some inner strength to fall back on, and above all, I had the entire staff of a whole department of a great hospital. I was the sailor. They were the boat.

YOU DON'T CHOOSE your decisive moment. It comes to you through an unknown force, and it's startling to realize that when it happens, the things that you had thought were important are not the ones that matter now. A dusty road in Colorado, a stroll with your father along a boulevard lined with sidewalk vendors, breakfasts with the children in the kitchen, a sharp turn in a car on a street in upper Algiers, a smoke-filled recording studio in a London suburb. What was it about these incidents that caused them to return to the surface during my decisive moment? And what can one say, then, about those endlessly unfolding blue forests? The answer will come to me, in the end, a little further along.

I've just written, "an unknown force." What does that mean? While rereading certain passages in Balzac, I discovered something interesting. Several times, when the novelist will not—or rather, cannot—explain what is at the origin of certain actions or feelings, he uses the same words: "I know not what power." He is careful to avoid speaking of God, of whom he speaks elsewhere, all through his *oeuvre*. But he doesn't trot out God when he wants to tackle the inexplicable—what surpasses our intelligence. What changes the course of our lives.

And so, rather than employ spiritualistic terms, rather than try to define what is indefinable, this "why" that Doctor D. and his colleagues are no more capable of understanding than are you or I—Balzac resorts to this practical and all-purpose expression, which suits me perfectly as well, and which I shall encounter several times in Room 29 (third floor, on your left): "I know not what power."

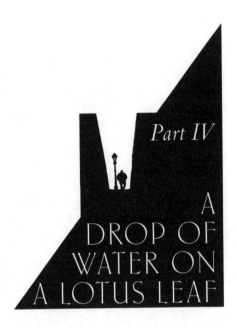

Part IV

A
DROP OF
WATER ON
A LOTUS LEAF

41

It Doesn't Matter

I LEFT THE ICU FOR ROOM 29.

Bare, light-colored walls. A tiny room, clean and impersonal. Freshly painted, a gray-and-white color scheme, like the floor, the wing, the entire recently renovated building. The room has been disinfected to eliminate any risk of germs from the previous occupant. For the first forty-eight hours, the strong odor stings the eyes, blurs one's vision, sets off migraines. But it doesn't matter.

There is just enough room for my bed, an armchair (in case I manage to get up), and a chair for a visitor. A small table for reading, writing, and eating just fits into the limited space between the bed and the wall. There is a bathroom, as cramped as the rest of the room, but as convenient and functional, too. I can get to it with some effort, leaning on the furniture and the walls, and I spend long minutes in front of the mirror staring at an unrecognizable face: thin, haggard. But it doesn't matter.

A narrow window looks out onto the courtyard of the pulmonary pavilion. From my bed, I can barely glimpse a simple scrap of sky, notched by the sloping brick roof of another wing of the building. Not a particularly rich perspective or landscape. But it doesn't matter.

One sleeps very little and very badly in a hospital, everyone knows that. The days are long and begin before dawn. There is always a neon light on, right outside the door. There are always patients pushing call buttons that go beep-beep in the night. There is always a feeble cry from some old man or woman repeating, "Nurse, please . . ." There is always the sound of the carts trundling supplies, medications, meal trays. There is always this hard bed, these yellow sheets bordered with a green material like some kind of paper. There is the nurse who wakes me up quite early because I have to take fourteen different capsules, one after the other, two hours before I can have any breakfast. There is sometimes a constant parade of people arriving for specific reasons: temperature, blood, weight, X-ray, inhalation therapy, rounds by the resident and the interns—it never stops!

It never stops, but it doesn't matter.

It doesn't matter because I know that I have reached the riverbank and left those dark waters behind. I can feel a new rhythm, slow and gentle, to which my body and senses will adapt. I feel that I'm relearning everything. The most elementary functions: eating, drinking, walking, peeing, washing, shaving, doing things on my own, using my hands and arms, reading. It's tedious, and very tiring, but it doesn't matter. I realized, from my earliest days and nights in Room 29, that it doesn't matter, because I know I will be leaving here. I know that Room 29 is only a temporary stop along the way.

42

Accepting and Rejecting
the Hospital

HOW TO MAKE GOOD USE of a hospital: a few new principles.

I quickly understood that I had to adopt a double attitude toward hospital life. One must accept it, and in the most disciplined, organized, flexible way, submitting to all constraints and directions. One must pay attention to what is required, prohibited, strongly advised. Carry out to the letter the instructions of doctors, nurses, and aides. Respect schedules, observe limits. Try to behave as much as possible like the "ideal patient." Smile and be lovable—in other words, worthy of being loved. Thank people for the most everyday gesture; for any service, no matter how often they perform it; for every effort, no matter how ordinary it is. Hospital life would not be livable otherwise. Always remember that you are dealing with people of whom much is asked and to whom little is given. And who deserve consideration.

The patient is an egotist, a spoiled child who expects everything, who is one hundred percent "on assistance." Well, the young woman who brings in the first meds at six in the morning, and the young woman who brings the breakfast tea and toast at eight, and the young woman who comes at nine to sweep the floor and clean the bathroom sink and wipe down the closet doors, and the young woman who comes at ten to set up the nebulizer treatment or to take the patient's temperature or a blood sample, and the women who come at eleven to change the bed linens and draw sheet—all the men and women who work tirelessly in this factory of life that is a hospital deserve your appreciation and your compassion.

This appreciation and compassion come all the more easily to you when you have been in the ICU. It's important to hold on to this feeling and to keep it heartfelt. Nurses, interns, therapists, the cleaning staff, supervisors, aides: they are just like you and me. They ask themselves the same questions: What are we doing here, in this life? What am I doing in this body? They even know a little better than you and I that we all must die, and that this knowledge makes us different from every other living creature on this earth. Even if they have never read it, they know a little better than you and I the truth of the Sanskrit text that tells us, "Life is precarious, like a drop of water fallen on a lotus leaf." And since they face this fact year in and year out, they have no doubt accepted it a bit better than you and I have. This doesn't mean that they aren't fellow human beings, fragile and vulnerable. Just because they're perpetually rooting around in your sheets, your hearts, your behavior, your whims, your fears, your recriminations, and your petulant demands, it doesn't mean that they don't deserve a bit of respect, kindness, and interest, like everyone else.

Who are they? What do they do when they leave this big factory? What do they read, if they read? What do they watch on TV? What do their children do? Where will they take their vacations—but have they enough money to go away on holiday? What movies have they seen—but have they enough money to go to the movies? Who are these anonymous, underpaid workers whom their nation ignores, yet whose job it is to take care of this nation? Who are these workers, scorned by their country? A nation that ignores, despises, and underpays its nurses, police officers, researchers, and teachers is a nation in danger.

AT THE SAME TIME that you must accept hospital life, and love those who make it possible (first principle), you must reject this life with all your energy (second principle).

You have to "dehospitalize," "demedicalize," "deinfantilize" yourself. From the very beginning, you should set out on the road back to independence. You must gauge your own strengths and weaknesses so that at the first sign of assistance, you can tell the person in the white coat who is offering to help you, "Thank you, but I'll do it myself. Thank you very much, but this is something I think I can do on my own."

Because there is nothing more dangerous, more tempting, and

more degrading than to settle into the comfy convenience of hospital routine. You must refuse to become a professional patient, refuse the great French national perversion: going on assistance. In the same way as you battled death and demons and insanity, you must fight off something even more insidious, seductive, and commonplace: retreating into a cocoon. Surrendering responsibility. There are patients who are too patient. There are hospital junkies. You have to approach the relearning of your basic skills with the stamina and willpower of great explorers who advance into virgin territory and never look back. Every minute of every day must be a struggle against lazy dependence. Just as a prisoner daily keeps alive his hopes of flight and freedom, a hospital patient must plan each day for his release, his lucky escape.

There is, however, one slight difference: the comparison is too simplistic, since a hospital is not a prison. And Room 29 is not a cell. It was in that room that I experienced several forms of absolute happiness.

43

A Postcard from California

THE FIRST HAPPINESS is that of being born all over again. A rebirth.

You rediscover things you were so used to that you couldn't imagine them being a joy. Like the power of speech. When you've been unable to speak, when you've believed that your larynx, palate, lungs, your whole respiratory system has deteriorated so badly that you will never speak again, this simple, natural act astonishes and delights you.

So I talk and talk. Too much. Doctor D. has ordered me not to "overdo it"—and I listen to him, of course, but I can't help it; I have to talk. They have installed a telephone for me to the left of the bed, on the little table I use as a minidesk. In a Rolodex are the names of everyone who telephoned in my absence, calling my family or my office to find out how I was doing. No longer "tongue-tied," I'm reestablishing contact with the outside world, with my little world.

The words come from deep inside me, from the center of my

body; I feel them rise, pass through my throat, reach my lips, my tongue—and I reel them off in amazement. Hearing yourself say the most ordinary words, tell people things, thank them (for letters, encouragement, get-well wishes), and ask questions (about them: How are you? And your family? What's new with you?) is a real joy and achievement.

Talking is listening to what others say, too.

My mother is on the phone, in Nice; when I was in critical condition, my brothers didn't tell her how seriously ill I was. Her voice brings me her face, her unquenchable curiosity—that frail voice in which I see her smile, her eyes, the way she moves around the balcony overlooking the Bay of Angels, the voice that sends me her love and kindness, the voice in which I hear once more the words and sounds of my childhood, and it seems to me that her voice hasn't changed since those evenings when she read Victor Hugo to us, or recited poetry, or sang us her little Christmas carols . . .

Then, on the answering machine: the voice of one of my oldest friends. We don't see each other often enough, but I have known and loved him since we were twenty, since our "débuts in Paris," and I feel something later confirmed for me by the sailor who rounded Cape Horn: "An irrational desire to talk to people whom you haven't seen for quite a while." My friend isn't home. I want to leave a little memento of my call, so I sing, in a very poor imitation of Yves Montand,

> *La voilà qui revient*
> *La chansonnette . . .*
> [Here it is, back again,
> That funny little song . . .]

And I'm "happy," as the sailor said. I know that this evening, when Pierre gets home from his poker game or from his dinner at La Vieille, he will listen to my song and feel relieved.

Singing. Talking. Making sounds. And touching. Touching my children's skin, my wife's cheek, her hair, her hands, stroking the curve of her neck. I'm not allowed to kiss anyone yet, and when I have visitors, they must still wear the white gauze masks that protect against any possibility of reinfection. But I can discover anew the skin of those I love, touch them lightly, make contact with life. Soon I will be rediscovering scents and smells as well, and the smallest bouquet of flowers in my little room will bring me another kind of wonderment before the myriad treasures of its petals, stems, and leaves. The tiniest stalk or leaf will begin to matter to me. And during those hot June nights, the bouquet will have to be removed from my room so that I can sleep.

But I wasn't sleeping. And that was another form of happiness. A happiness composed of solitude and silence.

IT WAS JUNE, during the longest days of the year. The light lingered until around ten o'clock in the evening. It was quite hot in

Paris, and I couldn't open my window until late, at the precise moment when the red, orange, and violet hues of the sunset were melting into the spreading indigo blue of night.

A touch of cool air would finally waft into the room. At that hour, the hospital switchboard no longer passed along calls. I could telephone out, but people couldn't reach me. I would have a last conversation with my wife and children, and then, I knew that the night belonged to me until the first noises of the morning out in the halls, before daybreak, before the first round of medications.

I would walk carefully to the open window and lean out to hear, drifting around the entrance pavilion, the sounds of cars along the Rue Saint-Jacques, a sound like silk tearing in the night. I would imagine the crowded café terraces on the Boulevard du Montparnasse, not far away; the Jardin du Luxembourg with its trees in their glossy, luxuriant foliage; and Saint-Germain, also close by, with that gentle, insouciant effervescence of men and women glorying in the intangible ephemerality of the moment. I would listen to the peaceful, indolent murmur of the city and, gazing up at an almost unpolluted sky of dark blue studded with stars, one of those lovely summer skies, I would have the feeling, despite the narrow window and the banality of the building partly blocking my view, that I was staring up into the blue firmament, into the heart of the world.

Then I would think about a postcard I had just received from California. It was a message from the wife of my friend Guy A. She and her daughter, Sasha, had been inside their spacious house in

Sherman Oaks when the recent Los Angeles earthquake struck. Mother and child had seen walls, furniture, roofs, facades, paintings, lamps, appliances, tools, and utensils sent flying. They had rushed down stairs that collapsed behind them. Everything was crumbling, cracking, toppling in jolting chaos, and they had found themselves out in the street in their pajamas in the middle of the night, saved by their mad dash and their immediate decision not to take anything whatsoever with them. They'd had the presence of mind, given the severity of the cataclysm, to flee without a moment's hesitation. To flee toward the only safe place: outside!

Guy, who worked out in the desert of Palm Springs, a two hours' drive away, had raced home along the freeway and found his family sitting in the avenue, right on the asphalt, between the rows of shattered palm trees. Sasha had been curled up in her mother's arms, in this once laughing and luxurious neighborhood that had seemed like a picture-perfect paradise—green, tranquil, neat, attractive—and that now resembled a movie set in ruins.

"We've cheated death," said the message on my postcard. "Guy told me what happened to you. I'm thankful that I saw my life pass before my eyes in a brief instant. We must seize that instant and weigh it carefully." On the front of the postcard was printed, in English, "Now that my barn has burned down, I can see the moon."

Looking out my window at the moon, I thought of something a woman had said during a dinner party I had attended. She was telling us how she had tried to drum some sense into a friend of hers, one of the most powerful men in the country—a wealthy, success-ful man who was incapable of slowing down, who was always do-ing, making, traveling, buying, selling. She had said something trite and simple to him: "Learn to count the stars."

At my little window, I kept gazing at the moon and I began to learn how to count the stars.

44

Early-Morning Tears

THE CITY GROWS QUIETER STILL. Traffic thins out. The breeze
is more refreshing.

Leaving the window, I sit down on my bed to read other messages I have received during the day. People have brought me news-
papers, too, which I have opened, glanced at, and immediately tossed
aside. I can't manage to read. There is a television in the room; I
don't watch it. And so, everything that had once passionately interested me—the course of events; yesterday's, today's, and tomorrow's
news; that bustling throng of men and women wrestling with a
world in constant ferment, with the immense futility of modern life;
rivalries, victories, murders, and wars; all that had once commanded
my rapt attention and reflection as a journalist and "media executive" every day of my life—now leaves me unconcerned and melts
away into the indifference of a cool June evening. On my first day
in Room 29, when my wife had asked me what I needed, I had told
her, "Some music, and some poetry."

As soon as I get my hands on Schubert's *Impromptus*, played by Brendel, I pop the disk into my little portable CD player, and for a long while—I have no way of knowing how long—I let the notes seep and sink into my body. I feel as though I have never before been able to listen to music so intently. In the concert hall or elsewhere, some thought or worry or incident would always distract me, and I would never fully succeed in absorbing the music, no matter how good it was or how fine the performance. I supposed that this was a failing, an inability to abandon myself completely to beauty. And now, late one June night, with the headphones jammed into my ears, I have surrendered to music for the first time and am enveloped in sound.

I experience the same phenomenon when I begin reading a poem: the words, the verses, their cadence and structure affect my mind with a particular intensity, making the images evoked more striking and memorable. As though I had acquired an enhanced ability to distinguish, retain, and enjoy what is beautiful. To remain undisturbed, undistracted. To delight exclusively in what I am enjoying, while I am enjoying it. I remember that strange way in which I struggled against the temptation of resignation, and death's invasion of the ICU, by reciting snippets of poetry in my head when I was practically delirious.

"If the very first things you ask someone to bring," I tell myself, "are music and poetry, and if you feed on them so greedily, it's because you wanted to regain what you missed the most, aside from your loved ones—what you were afraid of losing and felt slipping away, along with the breath of life: a need for beauty and harmony."

And I fall asleep. And when I awaken in a few short hours, I will know an even greater happiness.

IT WILL BE the ultimate form of happiness in Room 29.

It's not yet six in the morning. Through the half-open window, I hear a bird chirping. What is it? A sparrow? A little Parisian sparrow? I open my eyes. I see the sky, the hankie-scrap of sky peeking out from behind the edge of the redbrick roof in the narrow window, and I watch it slowly turn from blue-black to a thinner, lighter blue that will gradually become clear and luminescent. And I experience a long, salutary state of grace I find difficult to define except as a kind of ecstasy. Yes, I am ecstatic, and I begin to cry.

I weep slow, tender, and abundant tears, without sobbing, holding nothing back. It is the plain, ordinary spectacle of this peaceful dawn that delicately opens the floodgate of my tears. I have no thoughts, no reflections, no questions. Nothing else is going on inside me. I feel like a baby washed in the water of life.

"I know not what power" has brought me to this state. These tears of silent gladness, this feeling of absolute renewal, of seeing with fresh eyes everything that is so pure and simple in the dawn of a summer's day—I will experience this several mornings in a row like a ritual. It will be like a prayer of thanksgiving, the solitary and silent celebration of my rediscovery of this triple truth: The sun rises. The sky is blue. Life is beautiful.

IT IS ONLY natural that I did not die ten or fifteen days earlier in the ICU, since I had not fully grasped these three facts. Until now in my life, I had not yet performed this gesture of humility, this act of acknowledgment: weeping before the mystery of dawning light. And it was thus impossible for me to confront that other enigma: the mystery of dying light. I was not ready.

I'm not any more ready today, since I am alive and revived and regaining my strength, since I am lucky to have better understood the importance and worth of every moment and will not—for the moment—be looking behind me. But I tell myself that if the same thing happens again (and I well know that it will), then I will doubtless be a little more prepared, better armed, more able to chase away fear and face the moment of the final crossing. But on this particular morning, on the five or six mornings following that soft and lovely night in June, the mornings of fine ecstasy, I simply think, "You could not die because you had not experienced this."

An Apology to Six Teenagers

HE WALKED A LOT now, and for long periods of time. He did this every day, going farther each time. He would put on some lightweight trousers and a sports shirt, and slip his bare feet into a pair of worn Docksiders with yellowed laces. Telling the nurses that he was going for a walk and would be gone at least an hour, he would venture all the way down the stairs to the courtyard and then set out to wander through the hospital the way he did every afternoon.

He headed first for Radiology. He strolled around the little gardens, lingering in front of the small newsstand near the admitting office at the Rue Saint-Jacques entrance. He sat in the sun on a stone bench, watching a stream of visitors, patients, and staff members in their white coats—French-born Arabs, blacks, whites, women and children, and he could easily distinguish between those who did not belong to the hospital and those who, like him, would soon be going back to their rooms. Then he stood up to resume his tour of the premises, as though he were exploring a village. He knew all its streets, squares, intersections, and even the underground passages through which one could go from building to building without seeing daylight.

He finally came to the concrete ramp and metal railing sloping down to the entrance of a pavilion identified (in white letters on a red background) as the Intensive Care Unit.

"That's it," he thought. "For three weeks now I've been waiting to grow strong enough to come back here."

He hadn't stopped thinking about the ICU ever since moving to Room 29. He had walked past it more than once, but hadn't felt up to entering that place where he had lain "at death's door." A few days earlier, Doctor N. T. had accompanied him back to his room from Urology, walking slowly in the brilliant June sunshine.

Pointing to the ramp and the ICU sign, the doctor had asked, "Have you been back there? Have you seen the nurses again? You know, they appreciate that sometimes."

"I know," he had replied, "I'd really like to, but I haven't gotten all my strength back yet."

"That is where you experienced *distress*," Dr. N. T. had said. "That is the precise medical term that you should use and understand. You were plunged into respiratory distress, and it will take some months before you're fully recovered."

"It's a medical term?"

"Yes, that is what happened to you and that is where it happened, in there." And Doctor N. T. had gestured again toward the ramp, the walls, and the glass doors of the ICU.

But a few more days had passed before he had felt ready to push the buzzer at the entrance to the ICU. Now he knew that the day had come. Because he was doing well, doing better and better. He had regained a few pounds; he could feel his muscles coming back, and his legs; his breathing was regular and deep. He had been told that very morning to start thinking about going home at the end of the week.

The news had cheered him up. He felt it was high time to leave Room 29.

He had received all sorts of visitors. He had spent mornings answering every one of the dozens of letters from his colleagues at the radio station. He had seen his brothers again, and a few close friends. He had done a great deal of hugging and thanking and smiling and talking. He had listened. He had begun carrying out the plan that had unfolded magically before his eyes when he had come out of the anesthetic after his extubation, the plan telling him what he had to say, and to whom. The things he had to correct and change. A kind of "last wishes" list, but in reverse.

This was why he had made a certain appointment he considered very important. He had asked his fifteen-year-old daughter to stop by after school with her five best friends. The weather had been even warmer and lovelier than on previous days, so the girls had shown up in jeans and T-shirts or blouses. He had sat down on the stone bench in the courtyard, beneath the window of his room, which would have been too small to hold all the girls.

The school year was almost over; the classrooms were being used for exams, and the teachers were growing more and more lax and inattentive. The girls divided their time between school and long sessions of drinking Cokes at sidewalk cafés or trooping off to one another's homes. They had arrived after lunch, which they had eaten in the Jardin du Luxembourg, sitting in the chairs around the basin, and a last trace of these carefree moments still showed in their smiles and relaxed bearing, along with their captivating adolescent grace. They were a little band of friends, constantly in touch with one another through their endless daily phone calls, always hanging out together, something he had never done at their age. He had started chatting with them about the coming summer vacation, the movie they were going to see that evening. Sitting among them, he had noticed a look of mild interrogation in his daughter's eyes: "Why has Papa asked us all to come here?" The others seemed to be waiting for an answer. Friendly, rather silent, if not intimidated; on their guard, in any case.

"I wanted to see you because I owe you an apology," he had told them at last. "I wasn't nice to you this winter whenever you called my daughter and it was I who picked up the phone. I was cold and brusque, my voice was harsh, and I gave you the impression that you weren't welcome, that you were a nuisance, and that I didn't like you calling your friend so often. I'm afraid I might have given you a bad impression, as though I didn't like you, and above all, as though I were judging you, as though I didn't think you were good enough for my daughter, as though I were rejecting you, and I fear I might have hurt your feelings, yours and hers. That's why I wanted to see you, so that I could ask you to forgive me. I'd like to offer you a few explanations and excuses: I was already quite sick, but I didn't know it, not really. I wasn't aware that something destructive had invaded my body and was sapping my strength, attacking my life, and as it was doing so, changing my character. The crabby father you spoke to on the phone was a mistake—it wasn't really me."

Smiling, they listened to him quietly, and he experienced the same sensation he'd had in the ICU: the feeling that he could be outside his own body, floating overhead, watching himself go about his life. He thought it made a pretty picture, the six girls in their summer clothes, in their summer happiness, gathered around a man sitting on the rough stone of the bench in the little garden, apologizing to them. Trying to put things right.

"So, that's it. I just wanted to tell you that I love you and hope to see you at our place as often as possible. And hear your voices on the phone as often as you like. I love you as you are, each one of you, for your differences and similarities. You, Rapha, with your bright eyes and your wise perception of grown-ups; you, Natacha, whom I saw show such courage after a bike accident, impassive in the face of truly painful suffering; you, Sibylle, with your gaiety; you, Émilie, with your slightly melancholy air; and you, Katia, with your mischief, inventing words and expressions that make us laugh when our daughter repeats them to us at home in the evening. Thank you all for coming. I'm going to give you a kiss and send you on your way, because you've got lots better things to do on such a beautiful day."

His daughter, who was the last to embrace him, looked on placidly while the others kissed him good-bye, and without a single word they returned to the sunshine and the lindens of the Jardin du Luxembourg, to the promise of those pristine moments that made their retreating figures quiver imperceptibly with anticipation.

Death Is Not an Enemy

THERE HAD BEEN many conversations with other adults: discussions of projects, political and literary life, illness, images and feelings he didn't dare talk about at length, things he needed to keep private while he tried to understand them better. But although he didn't quite know why, it was his meeting with the teenage girls that had brought him the most satisfaction. He hadn't said anything particularly original to them, and he wasn't convinced that they had attached the same importance to his little speech as he had, but he felt that he had truly begun to display that tolerance and understanding he hoped to show in his relationships with others from now on, more generously and sincerely than in the past.

And then there had been something more impalpable: the image of those sunny young girls and the sweet gravity of their attentiveness. It had been a moment as fragile and random as those brought to the surface of his pain by his distracted memory during that ICU crossing—but perhaps as meaningful, too.

THE SAME WAS TRUE for each visit from his twelve-and-a-half-year-old son.

He had eventually learned what had happened on the Monday after his admission to the hospital, which wasn't very far from his son's school. After class, without telling anyone, the little boy had crossed a busy intersection and entered the hospital complex. Such a young child cannot, as a rule, go into a hospital on his own, but the boy had slipped past all barriers, avoided all inquisitive glances, and gone to the information desk on the floor where his father was supposed to be a patient.

"Your father isn't here," a nurse had told him. "He's in the Intensive Care Unit."*

Following the direction arrows, the child had found the ICU. He'd pushed the buzzer. He'd asked to see his father, and been told that this was impossible. He had gone back to school, but after classes were over, he had gone home, waited for his mother, and announced to her calmly, "*Réanimation,* that means you're not alive anymore and they're trying to animate you, to bring you back to life. So now I'd like you to tell me exactly what's wrong with Papa."

The boy was clever and capable. He had discovered a classmate with whom he had no particular ties of friendship but whose mother (he had noticed) held an administrative position at the hospital. Overnight, the little boy had taken a keen interest in this classmate, who lived (he soon learned) within the hospital compound itself.

---

*In French, the ICU is called *La Réanimation.* Trans.

From then on, the child assiduously accompanied his new bosom buddy home. Once his father had been moved into Room 29, the little boy, on the pretext of playing with his chum, would spend a few semi-illegal moments with his papa. The nurses never saw him slink by their station, and he would turn up between classes, at lunchtime. He would slip into the room, wreathed in shyness and affection, and take his seat in the visitor's chair, facing his father. They would chat about this and that: school, his pals, the opening scores of the World Soccer Cup in the United States. The child studied his father's slightest gesture, his least little breath, the severity of his cough (which was rapidly clearing up). When the boy gripped his father's forearm in saying hello or good-bye, the father understood that it wasn't simply so that his son could touch him, feel him, send him the message of his love through this fleeting gesture; the child could also judge the condition of his father's muscles in this way, and find out if he was gaining back weight and strength.

"Okay?" the patient would laugh. "You've checked me out? Feel better, now?"

There had always been these games of irony and feigned gruffness between them, that way of not flaunting their complicity.

"Oh, I'm not scared," the child had answered proudly. "I wasn't scared. I always knew you'd make it."

"How come?"

"Because I sent you secret vibrations."

The child had not said anything further to him about these "vibrations." Did he mean that after dinner was over, after he had done all his homework, when he was alone in his room, he had performed some kind of prayer, a brief meditation? Once, when he was only six years old, they had been walking barefoot together along the rocks on the point of La Castagne, south of Portigliolo, in Corsica, and the father had cautioned his son to be careful.

"Don't worry," the boy had replied. "I look first, I think it over, then I make my move. But sometimes I don't think, it just happens, it vibrates."

VIBRATION. During an entire decade, how many times had the laid-back apostles of cool trotted out this catchall word? After getting its start in California surfer music, then riding the hippie movement, and being recycled throughout the ensuing decades by all the cult pigeons, the guru groupies, the New Age suckers, the hawkers of pop psychology, the charlatans of inch-deep philosophies, the masters of quick-and-easy Buddhism or Zen in twenty-four hours, the deadly holistic quacks—the "vibe" had been served up in every possible way, and like so many words and images, it had lost all meaning. So he had distrusted it, made a point of never using it, just as he had tried later on to banish the adjective *fantastic* from his vocabulary when it achieved a sudden vogue fueled by songs and movies, becoming the stopgap of anyone at a loss for words. He hadn't always succeeded.

Now that his little boy had spoken of sending him vibrations, he remembered those waves of danger he had crossed in the ICU, the waves of love that had buoyed his resistance and helped him fight his way out of the black river, the waves of life that now coursed through him every morning at the cheeping of a sparrow, every evening when he saw, out in the hospital's small garden, a tiny blade of grass bending in the breeze that finally refreshed the seemingly becalmed universe of the hospital. And when he observed, while making one last round on foot through the silent buildings, the subtle transformation of shapes and colors, he readily welcomed the word *vibration*. And he reflected that when Balzac had fallen back on his, "I know not what power," it was because at that time, *vibration* had not yet been plucked from the chorus line of the dictionary.

The little boy had gone off to school again, leaving behind him in the room his small, personal vibration, like the one that trembles in the air after the ringing of a bell.

AMONG THE OTHERS who came to bring their "vibrations," there was the enigmatic yet candid Doctor T.

He would arrive unannounced at any hour of the day, with his motorcycle helmet under his arm, explaining that he would stay only a minute, but intent, focused, concentrating all his attention on the patient before him.

"You're doing better," he would say, taking his seat. "You seem calm, relaxed. That's good. Your eyes are brighter today, and more alert."

They had taken an immediate liking to each other, and were

quickly on familiar terms. T. would look over the care plans and temperature charts taped to the wall by the various nurses on duty.

"Everything's going perfectly."

"Yes, but is it safely behind me?"

"Absolutely not. You're by no means in the clear yet, and it will take some time before you are, but you're making progress. Now we must get you out of here so that you can ease back into a normal life again."

"Can life ever return to normal after something like that? I don't see the world with the same eyes anymore. I'm no longer interested in the things that used to take up much of my day."

"All that will return, slowly but surely. You must find a way to slip back into your daily routines and ordinary chores, get used to people and your professional obligations again, but you mustn't push yourself. Everything will come back, but you have been battling something serious, at very close quarters, and this will always make a certain difference deep down inside you."

He explained to T. that he no longer thought of death entirely as an enemy. At first, it had been an unknown, completely unfathomable. Then it had swiftly become a filthy trick, a mortal foe. He told T. that he had hated death; insulted, sneered, screamed, and laughed at it. Refusing to let himself be seduced by its siren call, by the second voice trying to convince him that he was finished, he had ranted and raved.

"That's because you weren't ready," replied T. "That was your way of fighting back, but it's also because you weren't ready."

After he had been through the black and white tunnels, the enemy had become, if not a friend, at least a more familiar notion—at the very time when he had felt a kind of peace spread throughout his soul, just before the extubation. He didn't think that it was resignation, because he had never fallen into the trap of being tempted to give up, but he had experienced something like acceptance. The end of a struggle. He had answered part of his own question.

"If I had crossed over to the other side, I don't know what I would have found."

"No one knows, that's just it! Sometimes I tell those who must be accompanied on a longer journey into pain than you experienced, especially those who will never return, that it's nothing: a quiet falling asleep. And then comes the beginning of the mystery."

T. stood up and consulted the pager that kept him in touch with his networks of friends and patients.

"Don't think about all that from now on. Life: you should think only about life, and those who love you."

"It's not much on my mind anymore. I'm alive, and what's more, I truly live each moment. It's wonderful."

"There, you see!"

And off he went, his motorcycle helmet under his arm, a messenger of friendship and a genius of comfort.

There Is No Korean Nurse
in the ICU

NOW HE WAS SITTING INSIDE THE ICU.

He had taken a seat at the large table in the center of the hall, around which, in his moments of lucidity, he used to see interns and nurses gather. Two nurses had joined him there now, drinking cups of coffee, and the head nurse had come over, too. He barely recognized their faces.

"How are you?" they asked.

"Fine, fine, and you?" he replied. "I wanted to see you and thank you, and say good-bye as well. I'm leaving in a few days, but I'll be back to see you when I return for follow-up tests at the hospital."

They hadn't much time to spare for him. They seemed pleased to see him, but there were patients to care for, patients calling out for them, and call buzzers and machine alarms going off. He had asked after Bénédicte, Florence, Patricia. They were off duty that day, so the others would pass along his greetings.

"And Karen," he had asked, "the pretty Korean?"

Elizabeth, the nurse he was talking to, had looked at him in some surprise.

"What Korean?"

"You know," he had said, "the one on the night shift—she's with another young woman who has a Béziers accent."

The nurses and their supervisor had stiffened, with skeptical looks on their faces and faint smiles of polite embarrassment.

"What are you talking about, *monsieur?* There's no Korean in the ICU."

He laughed and turned to the head nurse.

"No, really," he continued, "I didn't dream Karen up. I was even quite afraid of her, if you can imagine. I can admit it to you now, I thought you were all amazing. All your staff are amazing, Nurse, but there was something unsettling about her, she really upset me. Please don't misunderstand me, everything went fine, I haven't one complaint to make about her. She's certainly just as good a nurse as the others. But I don't know why, whenever she was taking care of me, I was much more restless, panicky."

The head nurse laughed, too, but announced firmly, clearly wishing to settle this matter, "Listen, *monsieur*, I assure you that there is no Karen here. We have never had a Karen here, ever!"

"I'm not crazy," he insisted. "She was tall, with long brown hair, that slightly shrill voice Asians have, and her shift partner was from Béziers, I think. They were a strange couple."

This time the head nurse spoke even more peremptorily.

"We have no one from Béziers here, and no one from Korea, either. We do have a girl from Montpellier, Nathalie, who often teamed up with a Breton girl, Catherine. They were part of the night shift when you were here, in fact. I can show you the staffing schedule, if you don't believe me."

He had the feeling the women were growing impatient.

"No, no," he said, "I believe you completely, of course."

It was very hard for him to accept the truth of what the head nurse had said, however. Had he been that delirious? So all the scenes, all the dialogues, all the images of Karen the Korean had been simply fantasies, hallucinations? Were they caused by the painkillers, by his semicoma? But then, why would he have imagined those particular scenes and not others? Why had he dreamed up that woman, those dialogues, and not others? He couldn't make any sense out of that aspect of his nights. It would have been different if he'd had that vision only once! But he had seen and heard Karen many times: she had literally been a part of his life in the ICU and she had been on duty one out of every two days. Thinking back on it now, he could see her again, bending over his face to put the ties back or to "suction" him—that horrible, sordid ordeal. And even though he trusted the tranquil assurance of the supervisor and the other nurses, he couldn't believe that Karen hadn't touched his life. And his brush with death.

"May I see my room again?" he asked, out of curiosity, but also to change the subject.

"It's unoccupied at the moment. Go ahead, it's over there, right in front of you."

He crossed the hall and pushed open the door. It was a rectangular room, rather small, with a bed in the middle of it, and standing off to one side, the empty IV pole. So it was in this modest setting that he had rounded the Horn. In this antiseptic box that he had received his "visitors": the dead of his life. In this impersonal place that he had, several times, felt life ebbing away, felt himself falling into that endless hole, felt the despotic hand of death slap him repeatedly in the face, trying to bring him down.

He went over to the bed, lay down, and remembered the corner behind him, on his left, that place he could never manage to see, where death had waited for him patiently, confidently, ready to swallow him up. Now that he could move freely, he turned toward the left corner, toward the angle formed by the back wall and the one that ran along the corridor. He was not at all surprised to see only the bare floor, the empty space between the walls: immaterial, impalpable emptiness. Nothingness. Nothing. And its silence.

Leaving the ICU, returning to the sky, the activity outside, the comings and goings of men and women in white or green, the trembling business of life, he kept asking himself: Who was Karen?

CONCLUSION

A Valid Hypothesis
Concerning Karen

I'T'S JULY, NOW, MID-JULY, and the weather is still delightful. All of France is sweltering through the dog days; I keep hearing about the heat and humidity over the telephone ("Just unbearable"), but it's nothing like that here. Where I'm living, it's nice and cool.

I'M IN A WOODEN HOUSE in the middle of a forest in Normandy. It's wonderful. Convalescence. I listen to music and read the poetry that was brought to me in the Hôpital Cochin. When I'm not reading, when I'm not bicycling around to get back into shape, when I'm not eating or sleeping, I lie in the sun, gazing at the trees and undergrowth, at the oaks, birches, pines, and the Japanese *Ginkgo biloba* and Canadian maple planted by my wife.

Looking at these trees naturally makes me think of that powerful vision I often had in the hospital: the carpet of blue firs. I think I understand better today why, lying in the ICU, I kept seeing so frequently, out of all the places I've been, the setting that seemed the purest to me: the forests of the Uncompahgre. The place where I would have liked to be, to which I clung desperately. I believe that this sweeping expanse of blue firs was the most beautiful representation of life, of reality, of wind and sky, fullness and emptiness, color and form. And then, it was my youth, too, and when I felt death reaching out for me, I clutched at that youth. At eighteen, in Colorado, innocent and inexperienced, lying on the Eagle's Notch, I had come—without realizing it—to a place of harmony, where the world was at a point of equilibrium, and like all young people, I thought I was immortal. All my life, ever since those hours of oblivious innocence, I had sought—and sometimes found, and lost, and sometimes found again—that point of equilibrium. And I had continued to believe myself immortal. At the hospital, during that cat-and-mouse game with death, during that crossing back to life, for the first time I stopped thinking of myself as immortal. Almost losing the world had given me another balance point, and if I was holding on so tightly to that image of the blue fir trees, it was because my love of the world and of life was centered in and summed up by that vision, that experience, and that beauty. If my mind was focusing so much on that image, it was so as not to lose the desire for beauty, the love of life. And if I had such a need for the purity of the sky and the open air, it's because my body was being stifled and desiccated. Finally, when we gazed down at it, that "sea" of firs showed us how tenuous and insignificant the line is between life and death, which meant that death (our possible plunge into the trees) belongs to life (the rippling carpet of blue velvet).

The blue firs were life, the life instinct, the desire for life, which gave both my mind and my body the strength to fight.

But death—what was it? Who was it? Not simply that empty corner behind me on the left in my room in the ICU. Perhaps it was Karen . . .

JUST BEFORE I left the hospital, I visited the ICU one last time.

Here again is the universe of my crossing: the light boxes where X-rays are hung up for study, the electric clocks on the wall, the pigeonholes full of messages, the charts, the coffee cups, the boxes of medications, the bottles, the bags of plasma.

Why do I feel so drawn to this place? The girls are there, always busy, wearing their green scrubs without any street clothes underneath, with their ballpoint or felt-tip pens clipped to the neckline. (The pen—the most sought-after object in the ICU: "There are never any around! Will you send us some? They're much better than flowers or candy.") There they are, with their youthful vitality blooming just beneath the seriousness of their duties; with their modest bracelets and earrings, their ID badges pinned to their breast pockets; with their preoccupied, conscientious expressions, and that transparent candor you see in those on intimate terms with suffering. Taking a moment to answer your questions on the fly.

"Of course it's hard. This is the toughest place in the hospital to work; but why else do you think we chose it?"

With the ringing telephones, which they answer patiently, courteously: "Yes, *madame*, he's doing well, he's resting. No, *madame*, not until this evening." With that electricity in the air, that edginess in their language and gestures, because everything moves quickly here and everything is critical, everything counts. There is zero tolerance for mistakes. Because they live in a constant state of siege imposed by the urgency and unpredictability of the danger in their midst. The ICU: a crossroads of decisions, of heightened emotions.

"You loved us very much, but didn't you hate us a little bit, too?"

"How did you know?" I ask.

They laugh. "Because it's always like that."

I insist on seeing Catherine, the young nurse from Brittany who the head nurse had assured me several times was on duty during the night shift (Catherine, and no one else) to assist and take care of me.

"You're not going to start talking about your Korean again," says the head nurse, in mock severity.

Catherine arrives. Her face and appearance are familiar to me. She's a French girl, with slightly prominent cheekbones; there are no rings on her fingers. She is young, brisk, pretty, and in a hurry.

"Well, *monsieur*, how are you? So you're all set, you're going home tomorrow?"

She is of medium height, with short brown hair. Karen was tall and she had long hair. Catherine's voice is low; Karen's was loud. This girl wears only a trace of makeup, while Karen wore bright lipstick and all sorts of costume jewelry. These two young women have nothing in common: the real one and the other, the one I thought I saw and heard several nights in a row. Was Karen the incarnation of death, which had invaded Catherine's body and my hospital room like a grave robber in an attempt to snatch me away? To seduce me? It doesn't take me long to reject this hypothesis, but I do play around with it, and there is no reason why I shouldn't: Death's first name is Karen . . . Even if I know that I was subject to hallucinations while I was under sedation, they still mean something, every one of them. They all have a meaning—because I saw them, even if they did belong to the realm of the invisible. Every patient who has to go through what I did is given these drugs. But we don't all have the same visions, visitors, encounters. And I also strongly suspect that we don't all fall into those tunnels—just as I realize that some patients go even farther than I did toward the "other side."

This is another of the many principles of such a crossing: Do not seek the explanation for your confrontation with death in a simple list of hypnotic or narcotic drugs and medications. This would be too easy, too "reasonable."

49

Life Is Not a Word

THE FOREST where I am convalescing is not far from the sea. I take my first walk there one morning when few people are around on that long and empty beach.

The tide is out, and you can walk quite a distance. With each step I take, when I plant the sole of my foot on the sand, I can feel everything. The gamut of differences between moisture and dryness, between the firmest and most yielding of materials, from the coarsest grains in some places to the finest powder in others. Each step toward the water renews the sensual pleasure of striding across a surface that lay beneath the sea but a few hours ago, and that the sea will reclaim in another few hours' time.

The air is salty and clear. I breathe deeply, eager to absorb in a single breath everything alive and intangible around me, and I recall that tender poetic line by Marguerite Yourcenar: "And in your lungs, air, this handsome stranger without whom you cannot live."

How right she was to set the adjective *handsome* next to the word *stranger* like that! Because air is not a word. No more than life is. Life is not a word: necessity forced mankind to give words to these strange things, but enclosing mysteries inside words has never explained them. Can anyone explain to me even how thought itself works?

When I finally reach the sea, I feel more and more shells and pebbles beneath my bare feet: the endless indefinable debris—yellow, orangey, gray, black, tea-colored—stranded by the tide. I stop, and the rippling white froth at the water's edge licks my ankles. There is a particularly hard shell under one of my feet. I feel as though I could keep it embedded there and so be connected to the rest of the earth, the rest of the world. This presence of the shell beneath my foot as I stand gazing at the ocean, gulping down draft after draft of air blowing in from nowhere, while the gulls, driven by I know not what power, follow a course unknown to me—this presence is not even a mystery anymore, but a miracle. And then I suddenly remember a poem by Walt Whitman, a poem I studied almost forty years ago, thanks to a red-haired professor whose face and limbs had been deformed by a childhood bout with polio.

50

Professor Turner's Poetry Lesson

HIS NAME WAS MR. TURNER. We adored him.

His limbs were withered, his lips twisted, his eyes staring. He limped across the campus, barely able to carry his books and papers on his own, and there was always a student to help that pathetic figure lurching somehow or other toward the classroom, a puppet smashed by the unjust demands of existence.

But a short while later, when Professor Turner began to read Walt Whitman's poem aloud, slowly and lovingly, the very act of reading this poem erased all memory of the unlucky man's tics, handicaps, and infirmities. The sight of Professor Turner exhilarated by the force and truth of the poem left us amazed and almost ashamed. Amazed by the beauty of this text, and ashamed, because for a brief moment—brief, yes, but a moment nevertheless—at the beginning of the year, when we had met Turner for the first time, we had, with the cruelty of youth, mimicked the crippled man's gestures and grimaces.

But now Professor Turner recited to us—with the conviction

and fervor of one who knew how to recognize and accept suffering, and how to triumph over it as well—a text that was like a hymn of love to the miracle that is life. The lesson he taught us comes rushing back to me in its entirety at the very moment forty years later (in other words, an instant later) when my bare foot treads—to my delight—on a shell on a beach in Normandy, and I give thanks (to whom?) for being cured, saved, for having learned something, for receiving a gift that is not given to everyone: the chance to take the road from which few travelers return—and live to tell the tale.

Here is the poem:

> Why, who makes much of a miracle?
> As to me I know of nothing else but miracles,
> Whether I walk the streets of Manhattan,
> Or dart my sight over the roofs of houses toward the sky,
> Or wade with naked feet along the beach just in the edge of the
>   water,
> Or stand under trees in the woods . . .

Reciting these lines, rediscovering them in my memory, I feel as if they were written a century ago for this very moment, for all the moments I have lived. The sight of the sky over the rooftops, that is Room 29. The bare feet at the water's edge, that is what I am experiencing right now, in Normandy. Standing beneath the trees, that is my convalescence. Professor Turner gave each line its due, taking pleasure in saying such simple words, while we listened, captivated, to every syllable.

> Or talk by day with any one I love, or sleep in the bed at night
>   with any one I love,
> Or sit at table at dinner with the rest,
> Or look at strangers opposite me riding in the car,
> Or watch honey-bees busy around the hive of a summer
>   forenoon,
> Or animals feeding in the fields,
> Or birds, or the wonderfulness of insects in the air,
> Or the wonderfulness of the sundown, or of stars shining so
>   quiet and bright,
> Or the exquisite delicate thin curve of the new moon in spring;
> These with the rest, one and all, are to me miracles,
> The whole referring, yet each distinct and in its place.

He often stopped after those last two lines. He would repeat them to us—writing them in chalk on the blackboard as best he could, with the atrophied fingers at the end of the stump that was his only useful hand—and insist that we should grasp their full meaning.

These with the rest, one and all, are to me miracles,
The whole referring, yet each distinct and in its place.

He wore a garish green jacket, and his clothes were often of gaudy colors that clashed with his red hair and made his already unattractive figure into something truly grotesque, yet at the same time, touching. Because now that I think back on it, I suppose that his choosing these loud colors was another of his ways of thumbing his nose at death, of accentuating the joyful and extraordinary aspects of life. He would turn around to face us as he recited the end of the poem.

To me every hour of the light and dark is a miracle,
Every cubic inch of space is a miracle,
Every square yard of the surface of the earth is spread with the
     same,
Every foot of the interior swarms with the same.

Turner would pause briefly before the last lines, standing in front of us with an impassioned light in his eyes—and I do seem to remember tears there, as well.

To me the sea is a continual miracle,
The fishes that swim—the rocks—the motion of the waves—
     the ships with men in them,
What stranger miracles are there?

After a moment of silence, Turner would add, "Before we return to our study of this text, of its words, rhythms, choice of epithets, I'd like you to ask yourselves for whom these lines were written."

At the time, I was incapable of giving an appropriate answer to Professor Turner's question. I was eighteen years old, and it was impossible for me to understand why that solitary, ugly, handicapped man had tears of happiness in his eyes when he recited this poem. Walt Whitman, born in 1819, published this poem at the age of thirty-seven—rather young to possess such clarity of vision. Today I understand perfectly Professor Turner's poetry lesson—and his question, too, which meant, "Ask not for whom these lines were written: they were written for you."

They were written for me.

They were written for you.

Building a Fire in
the Summertime

AFTER RETURNING from my walk on the beach to the wooden house in the forest, and having my long daily phone conversation with my wife (who had stayed in Paris), and hearing the latest news of the children (who had already gone off to camp), I decided to build a fire.

THERE IS NOTHING more agreeable and luxurious than making a fire in the fireplace in broad daylight in the middle of summer. A good fire is fairly easy to build.

You start by placing several balls of crumpled newspaper between the two andirons. Next you add twigs gathered in the forest, or sticks, pinecones, strips of bark, branches broken in pieces. This is the layer of youth, of the least little things. Then, on top of this layer, you put solid, medium-sized logs, taking care to place them cross-wise—in threes, if possible—while leaving some space between each set. This is the layer of strength, of vigor. You light the fire. The layers burn, one after the other. First the young twigs. Then the thicker, denser logs. When this scaffolding is nicely ablaze, you have only to add ever thicker and heavier logs that will take longer and longer to burn, and you can even indulge yourself by selecting a few that are still a bit green. There is something entertaining and reassuring about the sound of moisture hissing and oozing from the wood as it burns. And now you can step back, seat yourself before your handiwork, and watch the fire.

In the spectacle of flames embodying the transience of all things dances the very image of life itself: beautiful, colorful, ardent, and erratic; delicate and dangerous, present yet elusive, concrete yet fleeting; a thing of curves and keen edges, rending space, striking out into the emptiness around it, entrancing and unpredictable, cruel and wounding, sometimes hesitant and sometimes imperious, something that must constantly be fed, revived, maintained, enriched, defended, renewed, and cherished for as long as the flames last, for as long as one can and should nourish the fire, until the last flicker over the last ember, until the last red glow beneath the gray cinders, until nothing remains but the still-warm ashes . . . And then begins, perhaps, the last and greatest crossing.

ABOUT THE AUTHOR

A journalist and filmmaker as well as a highly successful novelist, Philippe Labro is the author of *The Foreign Student, One Summer Out West,* and *Le Petit Garçon.* This is his first work of nonfiction.